"The work that Yusuf is doing in the world of sustainable development represents his commitment not only to the preservation of our planet, but to the preservation of our natural resources and providing equitable communities for all. He is equal parts humanitarian as he is innovator."

—**Peter Tokar,** *president and CEO of McKinney*
Economic Development Corporation

"Yusuf Amdani has been a part of ChildLife Foundation from the time when this organization was just an idea. His generosity and philanthropy have been crucial in realizing this dream to provide healthcare to the underprivileged. Today, ChildLife is treating 1.5 million children every year, free of charge, and this has changed the entire landscape of healthcare in the field of pediatrics."

—**Sohail Tabba,** *entrepreneur, leading businessman and philanthropist,*
founding trustee and vice chairman of ChildLife Foundation,
director of Tabba Heart Institute and Aziz Tabba Foundation

"I have known Yusuf for more than twenty years; he is a kind, humble, sensible, and generous human being … the world is incredibly blessed to have him."

—**Karim E. Qubain,** *general honorary consul of Japan, president*
of the Consul Association Corps in San Pedro Sula

"Leaders who are open to those in all walks of life show us that demonstrations of humanity win in any setting. This book lays out techniques to follow to open doors and generate success in locations around the world."

—**David Miller,** *vice president of Yarn Division, GK Global*

"Yusuf Amdani has always helped when needed, and we're grateful for his continued support. His book will be a great help for anyone with a heart to make a difference in the developing world."

—**Mary Ann Kafati,** *president of the Ruth Paz Foundation*

"Central America holds incredible opportunities for companies like GK that choose to operate within its boundaries, and in doing so increase the overall economy."

—**Daisy Pastor,** *general manager of Seaboard de Honduras*

"Yusuf's role and leadership in Honduras is a one-of-a-kind example of how to overcome the challenges related to investing in developing countries with excellence, world vision, and responsibility. He is one of the best assets that Honduras has."

—**Kenia Lima,** *founding partner and owner of ZaGo Solutions, former vice president of marketing and chief of staff at the Honduras Institute of Tourism*

"Mr. Amdani's enterprises generate vast employment opportunities that are critical to the local economy directly and indirectly. These jobs attract foreign capital and currency that aid in maintaining our country's international cash reserves."

—**Roger Danilo Valladares,** *president of Universidad Tecnológica de Honduras*

"Yusuf has served as a mentor and role model to so many, me included. Those that read his experiences will appreciate knowing that the journey—complete with its ups and downs—is worthwhile in the end."

—**Lenin Palencia,** owner and CEO of Grupo Amcresa

"It has been a joy to oversee GK Foundation, as it provides the opportunity to those in need that might not otherwise have a chance at improving their lives. I know that together we can do more, as collective efforts lead to great results."

—**Georgina Barahona,** director of corporqte affairs at GK Foundation

"I met Yusuf in 1998, when he came to Campeche with the intention of establishing a manufacturing center … during and after the installation of these facilities, his company instigated investments in other areas of the state, including service and production sectors."

—**Arturo May Mass,** former secretary of industrial development for Campeche, Mexico

"This is the book for businesspeople and policy makers who want to make a difference in developing countries but don't know how or where to start or implement. Yusuf Amdani's experience and commitment hold many valuable lessons, perhaps the most fundamental being the importance of building, molding, and empowering a team according to basic principles of decency, transparency, and empathy. It's not as easy as it sounds, but the successes described in this book and others in Mr. Amdani's business life show that it can work with remarkable success."

—**Kenneth Frankel,** think tank president, international attorney, and law professor

World of Opportunity

World of Opportunity

BRINGING SUSTAINABLE BUSINESS TO FRAGILE ECONOMIES

Yusuf Amdani

Forbes | Books

Published by Forbes Books, Charleston, South Carolina.
Member of Advantage Media.

Forbes Books is a registered trademark, and the Forbes Books colophon is a trademark of Forbes Media, LLC.

Printed in the United States of America.

10 9 8 7 6 5 4 3 2

ISBN: 979-8-88750-121-5 (Hardcover)
ISBN: 979-8-88750-122-2 (eBook)

Library of Congress Control Number: 2023906385

Cover design by Matthew Morse.
Layout design by Lance Buckley.

This custom publication is intended to provide accurate information and the opinions of the author in regard to the subject matter covered. It is sold with the understanding that the publisher, Forbes Books, is not engaged in rendering legal, financial, or professional services of any kind. If legal advice or other expert assistance is required, the reader is advised to seek the services of a competent professional.

Since 1917, Forbes has remained steadfast in its mission to serve as the defining voice of entrepreneurial capitalism. Forbes Books, launched in 2016 through a partnership with Advantage Media, furthers that aim by helping business and thought leaders bring their stories, passion, and knowledge to the forefront in custom books. Opinions expressed by Forbes Books authors are their own. To be considered for publication, please visit **books.Forbes.com**.

DEDICATION

From early on, my parents set an example for my siblings and me of hard work, strong faith, and helping those in need. I witnessed them live out a humble life filled with honesty, strong ethics, high morals, and daily discipline. My father was tenacious in his expectation that my siblings and I would receive high marks throughout our years of education. He also oversaw our participation in charitable activities starting at a very young age. My mother was a genuine, caring figure both for our family and the others in our life. It was in her nature to reach out, to serve, and to assist everyone as she was able.

My three children, Ayaan, Anaya, and Ayeza bring me a joy I cannot express. I am forever indebted to my gracious and supportive wife Bushra. Without her tireless and selfless dedication to our home and our children, I would not be able to focus on GK's business endeavors and ongoing social initiatives. Because of her attentiveness, our children and family have a solid foundation that mirrors my own faithful and sound upbringing. In her, I find happiness, fulfillment, and hope now and always.

Collectively the actions and attitudes of my parents laid a solid foundation for me and my own life. They instilled in me a sense of family, important skills needed for growing and maintaining businesses, and the ongoing awareness to help society at every level. From them I learned the best lessons in life that I carry with me to this day and will always hold dear. This book is dedicated to them.

C O N T E N T S

FOREWORD

When I reflect on the past decades of Honduran history, I see a shining light in the figure of Yusuf Amdani. Unafraid to land in a country buried in poverty and crime, Yusuf established a garment plant in the outskirts of San Pedro Sula in the 1990s. At the time, few investors ventured into Central America. Fewer stayed for any measurable length of time.

Except Yusuf. Rather than shy away or return to his home country of Pakistan, Yusuf settled in Honduras. During the years that followed, he carried on business operations and expanded to new areas. He made friends who grew to become like family, readily welcoming him into their homes on weekends and holidays. He extended jobs to workers who had little to no years of education, and zero experience with a steady paycheck. He reached out to improve conditions for the community, to give children the chance to study English in high quality institutions, to prioritize healthcare, to integrate sustainable practices, to paint a brighter economic and social picture for society.

To the people who touched his life, Yusuf presented opportunity. He showed them a way to learn and grow. He set forth an example of integrity and high ethical standards, along with a vision to create a better place.

Now, looking at the country of Honduras, I see that thousands of workers have improved their lives, thanks to Yusuf. Communities have flourished and developed. Honduran society has changed; rather than being plagued with its past, its people are benefiting from the chance to earn income, to invest in their futures, and to reach out in turn to help others. Migration levels have dropped, crime rates have lowered as incomes rise, and poverty has evaporated in the homes of workers who receive fair wages.

Certainly, our past holds other figures who have shared Yusuf's vision. José Cecilio del Valle, a Honduras politician, philosopher, and lawyer, recognized that opportunities to learn could make a positive impact. He stated, "Education is the first need of the country." The Honduran poet Roberto Sosa penned, "The poor are many and so— impossible to forget." Froylán Turcios, a Honduras writer, stated, "I will never forget that my first duty, always, is to defend the honor of my country, the integrity of its territory and its dignity as an independent nation."

Yusuf has exemplified all of these and more. By becoming a naturalized Honduran, he has shown how much he has believed in the country and its people—even during times when others doubted. As a result of his efforts, Honduras has developed and improved the chance to play at an international level. His practices can be applied to other countries as well. For Yusuf, it starts and ends the same way: with a heart dedicated to the people and a hand to help them up.

Gustavo Raudales, CEO, Real Estate, GK, San Pedro Sula, Honduras

Look at the world around you, and you'll quickly see that it's flawed. It can be natural to want to make it a better place, both for people who live here and the environment. However, it can be difficult to find an effective, lasting solution that drives positive change.

Certainly companies and individuals in the past have tried. Many have done great things for this planet and its residents. However, we would be remiss not to point out that these changes are often done on a small scale. In general there has been an emphasis on making an effort to help in developing countries. A growing business in a country that is not yet fully developed might be able to help one or two households each year, for instance. A retailer could contribute a portion of its profits, though that portion may be 1 percent or 2 percent, or even lower.

These low donations are, in many ways, understandable. Organizations and small businesses may not have a system in place that maximizes every dollar. There is also sometimes a lack of awareness about the goodwill that could be carried out. It's easy to focus on issues that seem more pressing to drive the business forward.

More than thirty years ago, when I pondered how to make an impact myself, I didn't have all the answers. As I founded a multinational corporation, which has headquarters in a developing country,

I learned quite a bit about how to operate in suboptimal conditions. I was continually eager to try out new strategies and seek tangible results. I could envision ways to make my surroundings better.

Though it took substantial trial and error to get to this point, I can now say with confidence that I have discovered, to a certain extent, the secret to creating a better working and living world.

It is by creating opportunity.

Several decades ago my colleagues and I did exactly that. My company GK began as a small place in a struggling territory in Honduras. Over time my team members and I developed a business model that created job opportunities. We focused on the textile and yarn-spinning industry to start. Then we branched into other segments, including real estate, lifestyle, life sciences, and technology.

Today GK creates turnkey solutions and ready-to-use facilities that have attracted top-rated corporations, including Fortune 500 companies, public firms, and global industry leaders. These clients hire local workers for their operating needs in developing countries. With this model more than twenty thousand direct jobs have been created—and those numbers continue to increase.

Alongside GK's growth, more work opportunities have become available. As a result employment levels in communities have improved. Both the economy and people's everyday lives have been upleveled.

Employees come first at GK and are treated like family. We offer higher-than-average salaries and give workers the chance to continue learning. We want them to improve their skills and encourage their professional development.

We've even taken this one step further with the GK Foundation, which we formed to help the community. The group aims to make a difference in the medical world, with better patient outcomes and satisfaction levels. It also strives to provide school opportunities to underprivileged children. The foundation distributes healthy meals to those in need and carries out sustainable initiatives as well.

I know that I'm not alone on this mission. The efforts I carried out can be replicated by others, including you. Starting is simple. It begins with a shift away from a mentality that thinks, "I'm only one person—I can't create a big change." It encompasses a realization that we are all capable of making a difference. As Aesop, the ancient legendary Greek figure, said, "No act of kindness, no matter how small, is ever wasted."

In the pages that follow, I'll share the story of GK and its impact, with the goal of helping you on your own journey. You'll learn how the company got its start, the ups and downs it went through during its early years, and how it expanded into different countries. You'll understand how it has genuinely assisted others in the community and changed their lives for the better. You'll also get a glimpse into what's ahead, including exciting opportunities in the technology industry.

It is my desire that we collectively paint a new landscape for the coming generations. My hope is that, after reading this book, you'll see the world as a place you can touch and change. You'll grasp how doing business in developing countries can be an all-around win.

In every chapter I've laid out strategies to maximize business opportunities in developing countries. They reflect the lessons I've learned from my own experiences. They include carrying out the research needed to find a location that is slated for growth. We'll also cover looking for ways to make a sustainable start. I map out paths to create a transformation and bring new industries to societies.

At every step I think it's essential to prioritize education. I share the ways GK has done this and how you can too. We'll cover how to provide medical assistance and work toward a greener future. We'll close by visiting the multiplier effect, which can occur when you build systems that elevate workers and partner with organizations that share your values.

At the end of the day, our objective should be to create opportunities where they are most needed. Making this happen may require leaving your comfort zone to find those territories. When you do, I can assure you the effort will be worthwhile. Together we can build businesses that thrive in developing countries. Along the way we can look for ways to improve societies and economies.

CHAPTER 1

Understand Real Impact

How do you generate positive change? What do you do in your community?
How do you act outside of your region or country of residence? How do
you address low-income areas, where the needs may be greater?

Perhaps you've opened this book to find out. Or maybe you have other motives. You might be thinking of nearshoring, building an overseas company, or testing out a new idea. Maybe you're looking for ways to create sustainable processes and use renewable energy. It's possible you're interested in partnering with a foundation to help others.

Regardless of the reason, I'm glad you're here. I have something to share, and I appreciate your attention. I have long wanted to improve areas of the world. I'm originally from Pakistan and have built businesses in Central America and other regions. To really make a difference, you need a specific approach.

To get started let's consider the type of change we want to create. The kind I look for runs deeper than occasional community events. It extends beyond raises and promotions. It goes further than annual giveaways.

The impact I seek involves real people. It aims to educate workers. It seeks to help low-income societies climb out of poverty. It works to expand the middle class, the engine of a strong economy. It brings new opportunities to regions that are often hidden or overlooked.

At every step the change encompasses sustainable practices. I aim to set up self-supporting hubs that provide their own energy. I look for ways to create more green and higher levels of beauty wherever I go. I establish a chain of aid in communities, including healthcare support, educational improvement, and nutritional provisions to those in need.

Along the way there are chances to partner with those who share these goals. These arrangements might be made with local hospitals, nonprofits, school systems, or community boards. I look for leaders who have values that align with my own company and philosophy. This typically involves building relationships with informed locals. It also includes steering clear of complicated government ties or unethical practices like bribes, which are typical in many developing countries.

The impact I seek involves real people.

To demonstrate how my company strives to make an impact, allow me an illustration. I'd like to invite you on a short trip. Consider it a preview, similar to a movie trailer. This tour will give you a taste of making a real difference. It will also portray what I believe are symbols of well-being in business and in life. Keep in mind that at GK we consider success to be measured not merely in financial terms. We also evaluate how much positive change has been carried out in the lives of others.

A Glimpse at Impact

Our mini excursion begins in my office in San Pedro Sula, Honduras. To get there, if you're not from San Pedro Sula, you'll have to first fly to the city or take other modes of transportation. With nearly one million people, this bustling place is the industrial center of the country.[1]

Once you're in the city, you'll notice several factors. First the metropolitan area reflects the economic status of the country. Honduras is the second poorest country in Latin America, after Haiti. More than half of its inhabitants live below the poverty line.[2]

As you ride through the boulevards on your way to my office, you'll see a juxtaposition at play. You'll pass main avenues lined with office buildings, shopping centers, and fine-looking restaurants. Then you'll turn a corner and find yourself in shanty neighborhoods and potholed streets. Waterways run through the city, as it is situated in the Ulúa River Valley. Along the channels, dilapidated shacks built from scraps try to hold their footings on the muddy banks. The residents pick fruit from the trees that line the river. Their days revolve around a search for food and survival.

In addition to the poverty level, you'll notice traffic, congestion, and an ongoing bustle. Many of the city's citizens are on their way to work, returning home from a job, or looking for employment. Hondurans with professional positions tend to put in long hours. However, this aura of hustle doesn't equate to high paychecks. Rather

---

1   Macrotrends, "San Pedro Sula, Honduras Metro Population 1950-2022," accessed July 20, 2022, https://www.macrotrends.net/cities/21135/san-pedro-sula/population.

2   World Population Review, "Poorest Countries in Latin America," accessed July 20, 2022, https://worldpopulationreview.com/country-rankings/poorest-countries-in-north-america.

their wages tend to be about a tenth of what is earned for similar employment in a developed country.[3]

Finally you'll notice levels of security at nearly every stop. Gated communities, guards at the entrance of buildings, and a skepticism among strangers—it's all here. In a sense it comes with the territory. In the past, Honduras gained worldwide notoriety for being called "The Murder Capital of the World."[4] Security is an ongoing concern for many in the area.

Upon witnessing these impressions, you may be wondering, *What am I doing here?* Let me assure you, this will be a safe, enlightening time. It's also important for you to be here. I want you to experience it, as I have.

You approach my office, which is located inside of Altia Smart City, the business process outsourcing (BPO) and information technology outsourcing (ITO) hub of Central America. The complex includes a business park focused on work-life balance and wellness. It's also home to GK headquarters.

Altia stands out as a sustainable ecosystem that pulses along to the heartbeat of San Pedro Sula. At the park, GK hosts international companies with outsourcing needs. These multinational firms come in and are given turnkey, ready-to-use or ready-to-lease facilities. GK takes care of everything. It covers the setup, the hiring, and the management of the operations. (For more information on Altia, head to chapter 4).

---

3   Jennifer Zilly, "Those of Us Working to Improve Life in Honduras Find the Caravan Troubling," Dallas News, November 2, 2018, https://www.dallasnews.com/opinion/ commentary/2018/11/02/those-of-us-working-to-improve-life-in-honduras-find-the- caravan-troubling/.

4   David Bacon, "If San Pedro Sula Is Murder Capital of the World, Who Made It That Way?" *The American Prospect*, June 13, 2019, https://prospect.org/economy/san- pedro-sula-murder-capital-world-made-way/.

I meet you at the door, because I'm on my way out to a quick meeting at Green Valley, an industrial hub that GK operates outside of San Pedro Sula. Back into the car we go. I note that we won't be away from the office for long and promise we'll end our tour back at Altia.

A Chance to Have a Hot Meal

It's nearly lunchtime. As we leave Altia, you notice two pickup trucks with the GK logo ahead of us. Each has several containers filling up the space in the back.

When you ask about their connection, I explain that these trucks work with our company's charity segment, which is called the GK Foundation. Every day around noon, the vehicles head out to a part of the city. They go to different distribution points. At these they hand out five hundred meals for free to anyone who walks up to the trucks.

This service is important to GK, though you may be curious that our first "business" encounter involves feeding the hungry. At our company this is a very important and valuable segment. Nutritional meals are prepared every day within the walls of Altia, the complex we just left.

Efforts to hand out freshly cooked food began during the pandemic, to help struggling segments of the population in Honduras. Surely you saw on your way in that many here continually search for nourishment. Some resort to picking through scraps or trash to find food.

At GK we provide meals every day. We go to different spots and deliver these plates of hot food. Individuals gratefully accept them. They share the dish with their families.

This activity takes on great significance when we look at the context. Honduras is an extremely poor country, and most of its residents cannot earn enough to feed themselves. There is, quite literally, no other short-term solution to provide them with the food they need. Those in poverty have extremely limited options to alleviate their hunger pangs. They have no solution for this calamity.

On the menu for today, I explain, are cooked chicken with vegetables and bread. The meal is served with a sealed plastic package of water. Rather than giving out sugar-laden beverages, an effort is made to provide clean, valuable resources. The food is cooked from fresh, local ingredients. It doesn't contain chemicals or preservatives. The overarching goal is to provide the highest level of nutrition.

Several minutes later the two trucks carrying food packages pull off to the side of the road. They slow down next to a row of huts made with metal and wood scraps. As soon as the vehicles stop, individuals from the neighborhood line up. The distribution begins. One by one, residents walk away with a packaged meal in a disposable container.

Children flock to the truck. Some mothers carry several meals in their arms. Adults tote the containers back to their one-room, rundown homes. There they might share the food with their aging relatives who are too crippled to come outside and get their own meals. Smiles abound from those that receive this burst of generosity on an ordinary day. They are about to partake in a hot meal, and it may be their only one that day.

High-Quality Healthcare for Free

Our vehicle moves on, away from the food distribution trucks. Several blocks later we pass one of the city's main public medical centers. It is called the Mario Catarino Rivas Hospital. There are swarms of people outside the facility.

Together we watch a family of four balanced on a motorcycle approach the hospital. The father figure drives the small vehicle. Two small children balance behind him, and the mother sits in back with her arms wrapped around the youngsters. One of the children's arms is in a cast.

The motorcycle pulls into the hospital area, maneuvering around pedestrian crowds to get through.

You ask why the place is so busy.

I mention it is an average day. Many of the patients have come from rural areas. The sick have arrived with their families, and together they wait to receive care. They might not be able to afford to commute back and forth from their home to the hospital. While treatment is provided by the government, there are often extensive lags in service. It's not uncommon to wait a year for an appointment with a specialist, or longer for a needed surgery.

We just saw GK Foundation handing out hot meals to those in need. Now you inquire if our nonprofit branch helps those with medical needs. In response I explain that within Mario Catarino Rivas Hospital, GK Foundation has a clinic called Love and Care. This place offers private-level quality of care at no charge. It is open for anyone and helps speed the process for treatment and recovery. (We'll look at this more in depth in chapter 8.)

This is part of our effort to collaborate with organizations that aim to improve conditions. Through our medical work, we extend high-quality care to individuals who can't afford medications or doctor visits. We provide services and treatments for free. We treat everyone with respect. Under these guidelines we help create healthy outcomes for low-income families. After they receive care, individuals can return to work. They support their families and have a higher sense of well-being.

Bilingual Learning

Just as quickly as it came into our view, the hospital is behind us. We move out of the city and speed along a highway that will take us to Green Valley. This is the industrial hub I started more than two decades ago. As we observe the rural area surrounding it, we notice it has a lower poverty level than the city. I mention that many individuals here are short on opportunities.

Some haven't had any education. Others have studied for at least a few years in school but don't have a long list of skills. If they attend public schools, they won't learn English. Public schools are free and available to all. However, they don't teach languages outside of Spanish.

While private schools in Honduras offer English training, the education comes with a price. For those living on a subsistent basis from day to day, paying for school is out of the question. As such, these individuals don't have a key asset—English—which could lead to a job opportunity after school.

This is the very reason that GK Foundation began working with public schools. It didn't seem like a level playing field to offer English at a price. To open doors for the upcoming generation, GK collaborated with public schools in the San Pedro Sula area. It offered to provide everything needed for a high-quality education. This would come complete with English language learning, and it would be available for free to anyone.

These schools are now up and running. Along our trip I point to a road that leads off the highway to one of them. It is situated in a small village a few miles from Green Valley. You ask if we can go there. I promise I'll take you to the place at a later point (in this case, chapter 6! In it we'll delve into GK's educational efforts in the region).

A Green Industrial Hub

As we pull into the industrial hub, we discuss its name. The area is, indeed, green—both in color and by environmental measures. I point out the solar panel project, which provides renewable energy to the facilities. I also show you the nursery, where all the plants and greenery for the businesses are grown. Throughout the hub, measures to create self-sufficient operations are in place. This is a reflection of our focus on long-term, sustainable practices.

I have to meet a client at its manufacturing facility in the hub. I invite you to come into the place with me. The tenant graciously gives us a quick overview of the site. He notes that a job at this plant provides an opportunity, up to a certain point, for the surrounding community. Employees of the company receive government benefits and a steady paycheck. For adults who didn't have the chance to finish their elementary education, this type of work provides a chance to move up. In many cases the other options include unemployment or microbusinesses, such as selling baleadas (a filled tortilla) on the street. A factory job brings more financial security than these other choices. (More on Green Valley in chapter 3.)

This setup coincides with our desire to create tangible differences in the lives of workers. We want to give them the chance to work and receive a salary. When this happens the community can begin its journey out of poverty.

The Chance to Uplevel

My meeting at Green Valley ends. We head back to Altia, the technology hub where our journey together began. Upon arrival at this place, which I mentioned also serves as GK headquarters, we walk toward my office. Along the way we pass a university campus, called Unitec.

You ask about a college located so close to Altia. Is it a coincidence?

No, I respond. In fact arrangements were made precisely to have Unitec, a well-known and prestigious university in Honduras, at Altia's side. The design provides a chance to offer further education for employees. If a worker needs additional training or wants to complete their university degree, the education is accessible. It is literally within walking distance of where they work. This upleveling of skills is a key aspect to GK's business model. It creates the chance for workers to move ahead and develop professionally. We'll study this topic more in chapter 4.

Living beyond the Dream

Once we're inside my office, the wait staff brings you a cup of coffee as our conversation continues. I mention there's more I'd like to share. The story of GK and its efforts to make a real impact reach further than we've just observed.

While it is gratifying to know that GK has helped to improve the well-being of its workers and the citizens in its area, I hardly imagined these results would take place when I first started. All I knew was that I wanted to make a difference.

At the beginning there were both business and social opportunities. I was convinced that I could develop win-win situations. If a company is strong and growing, it can find ways to better the community in a real, tangible way.

CREATING CHANGE FROM GENERATION TO GENERATION

Interestingly my own path did not start in Honduras. I'm originally from the city of Karachi in Pakistan. I come from a line of ancestors who have been active in business-related matters for generations. However, my relatives have always focused on more than merely deals and trades. For them the idea of doing business is deeply rooted in helping humanity. Their care and concern for others, along with their support for charities and meaningful contributions to society, were instilled in me from early on. These very initiatives that helped shape my mindset as a child would never leave me, even as I grew and matured.

Upleveling of skills is a key aspect to GK's business model.

For my education I studied at the University of Karachi and graduated with a business degree. I went on to get an MBA in marketing and finance. I knew that as I developed my own businesses and tread along my life path, I would follow in the ways of my family. An eye for humanity, a heart for the people, a passion for the vulnerable … these would serve as my vision for the future, just as they had guided my family in the past.

Some of my close family members have been involved in the textile and yarn-spinning industry for generations. As such, with an MBA in hand, I decided to pursue the same line of business. I wanted to go to a developing country that could easily serve international clients and be a nearshoring option for the US. I was also committed to going to a region where a positive impact could be made. My search led me to Central America. In the 1990s I chose Honduras as the best location.

I helped the family business to expand there. During the following years, my team and I worked to build up the company and branch into other countries. Today the corporation I founded, GK, has operations around the world. It's involved in the textile, real estate, lifestyle, technology, and agriculture industries.

IN THE SHADOWS

Spend a little time with me and you'll quickly see (as is evident in this chapter) that my preference is to discuss impact rather than my own accolades. I firmly believe that wherever my business thrives, it should bring significant benefits to its employees, the cities in which it is located, and the country where it operates. That's why I also created GK Foundation, which focuses on needs related to health, education, nutrition, and the environment.

Our mini tour has come to an end. However, the tale of how to do business in developing countries and make a positive impact is just beginning. I now invite you to read on to see how companies can indeed do well in up-and-coming regions. Just as GK has been able to make a difference for others, I believe anyone can make an impact. It starts with a desire to help.

In the chapters that follow, you'll learn the how-to aspects of creating positive change. The pages will equip you with everything you need to implement sustainable business practices and community-building initiatives. Let's move on.

HOW TO DO BUSINESS IN DEVELOPING COUNTRIES

- To create a true impact, we need to shift our mindset away from token gestures. Think beyond one-time, scattered, or small efforts. Look for long-term opportunities that can be carried out routinely and incorporated under the company's umbrella.

- Helping others takes on new meaning when we approach it holistically. Consider the overall well-being of people and the economy when looking for improvements. Account for nutrition, medical care, education, and income needs. Make sustainability part of your philosophy so it will guide your projects.

- Partnering with local organizations can create momentum and drive change. Look for collaborations where values are shared. Talk to community leaders to gain their insight on local needs.

- Making an impact starts with doing business well. If the company is profitable, it will have the resources needed to support and improve the community.

CHAPTER 2

Investigate Regions for Potential

When GK first considered establishing investments in Honduras, the proposition often caused eyebrows to raise. Setting up its headquarters in the country also led to inquiries. Those who heard of the plans tended to ask questions, such as

Why Honduras?

Where is Honduras?

Have you considered other places?

My friend and fellow reader, if you are having the same thoughts, I welcome the discussion. I believe it provides us an opportunity to explore the country I have come to consider home. Indeed I have invited many to come and enjoy it alongside me. Honduras has become a part of me. When I look around, I see a place filled with family, companions, and citizens whom I care deeply about.

Furthermore these questions open the door for a conversation on a deeper level. They allow us to think about the country in business terms, especially in economic and social standards. Honduras is considered a developing country. When inquiries are raised about moving and working here, it gives us the chance to explore the idea of investing in similar places.

To begin let's widen the lens and look at this topic from a global perspective. We'll consider how developing countries are defined and compare them to developed nations. We'll also observe the choices companies face when it comes to outsourcing, especially the decisions surrounding offshoring and nearshoring. We'll circle back to Honduras and answer those quandaries that are frequently presented when we talk about the country.

In each section consider the takeaways you can apply to your own research. Looking at statistics about a new country is a start. Talking to locals helps you gain insight into their challenges. Touring lesser-known regions could lead to findings that will support your business plan. You might discover an untapped labor pool, affordable land, and trade laws to help your company thrive.

Classifying Countries

Perhaps at a glance one can make observations about what it means to be a developing country and what it takes to be a developed country. Entities that have robust economies, lead the world in certain industries, and have high levels of income may be considered developed. A nation with a low standard of living and political instability might be classified as developing.

Interestingly the United Nations (UN) divides countries into three categories: developed economies, economies in transition, and developing economies. Its classification system accounts for weighted averages of country data. It includes economic growth rate factors like gross domestic product (GDP). It takes a long-term view, often accumulating data from the past ten to fifteen years.

In North America, the countries of Canada and the United States are considered by the UN to have developed economies. The

European Union, along with Iceland, Norway, Switzerland, and the United Kingdom, are also on the list. For Asia and the Pacific regions, the UN includes Australia, Japan, and New Zealand.[5]

Regarding economies in transition, the UN notes several countries in Eastern Europe, which are Albania, Bosnia and Herzegovina, North Macedonia, and Serbia. It lists others from the Commonwealth of Independent States, including Armenia, Azerbaijan, Belarus, Kazakhstan, Kyrgyzstan, Republic of Moldova, the Russian Federation, Tajikistan, Turkmenistan, Ukraine, and Uzbekistan. Georgia is also considered to be in transition.[6]

Moving on to developing economies, the UN marks nearly all countries in North America in this category. Only the US and Canada are considered developed. Every nation in South America is considered a developing country. Also listed in this section are Caribbean islands like the Bahamas, Barbados, Belize, Guyana, Jamaica, Suriname, and Trinidad and Tobago.

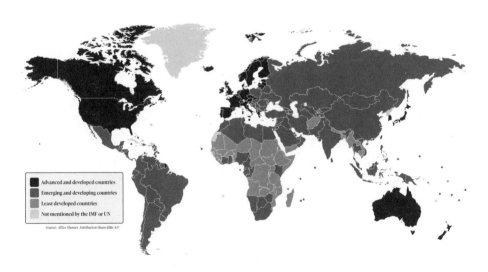

Advanced and developed countries
Emerging and developing countries
Least developed countries
Not mentioned by the IMF or UN

Source: Allice Hunter, Attribution-ShareAlike 4.0

---

5   United Nations, "World Economic Situation and Prospects 2022," https://www.un.org/development/desa/dpad/wp-content/uploads/sites/45/WESP2022_ANNEX.pdf.

6   United Nations, "World Economic Situation."

All the nations in Central America, including Honduras, are considered to have developing economies. In South Asia, we find India and Pakistan on the list, along with Afghanistan, Bangladesh, Bhutan, Iran, Maldives, Nepal, and Sri Lanka. There are countries from Western Asia like Bahrain, Iraq, Turkey, and the United Arab Emirates. Nations throughout East Asia appear, notably China, Hong Kong, North and South Korea, Singapore, Taiwan, and Thailand. All of Africa is considered in development.[7]

SEPARATING THE MOST AT RISK

In addition to these categories, the UN creates several subsets. One of them is referred to as the Least Developed Countries (LDCs). These are low-income countries that encounter severe structural barriers. The obstacles prevent them from achieving sustainable development.

LDCs have low levels of human assets, which are measured by looking at the rates of secondary school enrollment, undernourishment, maternal mortality, adult literacy, and under-five mortality. The countries are considered economically vulnerable, as determined by the sizes of their population, how far away their people live from access to resources, and their instability of exports. The UN also measures their number of victims of natural disasters, the share of agriculture and fishing in GDP, and the percentage of population that lives in coastal zones.[8]

There are forty-six countries that make the LDC list. Throughout the Americas, only Haiti is considered an LDC. The remaining nations come from Africa and parts of Asia.[9]

---

7   United Nations, "World Economic Situation."

8   United Nations Department of Economic and Social Affairs, "Least Developed Countries (LDCs)," accessed August 19, 2022, https://www.un.org/development/desa/dpad/least-developed-country-category.html.

9   United Nations, "World Economic Situation."

In another subset the UN lists nations it classifies as heavily indebted poor countries. Of the thirty-nine states, we find entities in Central America, namely Honduras and Nicaragua. Nations from Africa and Asia also appear on the list, including Afghanistan, Ethiopia, Rwanda, Togo, and Zambia.[10]

DECIPHERING THE DATA

What does this data tell us? I believe much can be learned from it. To start, it is an affirmation of just how wide and expansive the world is. When discussing investments it's true that it may be easy to focus on developed economies. In fact the G7 is often highlighted in discussions of the most advanced nations (the G7 consists of Canada, France, Germany, Italy, Japan, the United Kingdom, and the US).

When we consider the lists of economies that are in transition and developing, along with the subsets of LDCs and the most indebted, we can see the world extend before us. If you spin a globe and put your hand on its surface as it moves, you'll feel country after country whirl past. Of the 195 nations in the world today, the minority are considered to have developed economies. The lists for those in transition and developing are much lengthier.

Certainly there are reasons why developed economies tend to draw more global attention and take on leadership positions. They often hold resources and attributes that simply aren't available in developing economies. To clearly lay out the differences in terms of where to do business, it can be helpful to look at the advantages and drawbacks of both. We'll do that next.

---

10   United Nations, "World Economic Situation."

Doing Business in Developed Countries

When we speak of nations with developed economies, we are usually referring to places that share common features that go beyond their levels of GDP. Developed countries often have high living standards, stable birth and death rates, and low infant mortality rates due to the access to quality healthcare. Typically more women are found in the workforce, unemployment rates are low, and family sizes are smaller.[11] Education is readily available to children and young people. Academic accessibility reaches high school levels. Much of the population is eligible for university and postgraduate degrees.

Developed countries use a disproportionate amount of the world's resources. Their populations may depend on autos for daily transportation. Citizens frequently travel by plane for work or personal reasons. They use more electricity and gas to run their homes.

The latest technology is readily available and accessible in developed economies. Agricultural sectors are highly productive and may use automated machinery and systems to carry out the work. Many industries are oriented toward service and adding value. The working environment is usually regulated and run by a standard set of rules.

Due to the stability that you'll find in developed countries, companies find certain advantages to operating in them. Among these are a reliable infrastructure that supports their activities, an educated workforce, and the potential to use the latest advancements in technology. Firms don't often have to worry about power outages, political unrest, or a loss of their workforce to other countries.

When it comes to certain segments, including manufacturing, several drawbacks stand out. The costs for operating in developed

---

11 Investopedia Team, "Top 25 Developed and Developing Countries," Investopedia, May 27, 2022, https://www.investopedia.com/updates/top-developing-countries/.

economies is usually high, as workers often expect higher salaries and comfortable working conditions. They may request paid leave and ergonomic office equipment. Expenses tied to importing raw material or sourcing it locally may lead to higher costs of production. If these factors cause companies to raise the price of their services and goods to remain profitable, consumers may not be willing to pay more, resulting in poor market performance.

Doing Business in Developing Countries

When we survey countries that are developing, common characteristics stand out. These nations have less access to technology and lower levels of capital. Their rates of unemployment run high. They have lower standards of living. Overall they are considered not to have reached their economic and industry maturity levels. Industries may not be as regulated as they are in developed nations.

There is generally a stronger focus on agriculture, albeit with lower levels of productivity. Some or most of the population might carry out subsistence living, in which they have just enough food or money to survive. They frequently grow crops to provide for themselves and their families. Due to limited resources, these households are not able to sell or scale what they produce.

Crime and murder rates may be higher in developing countries. These nations are often crippled with political instability and concerns surrounding corruption. Unskilled labor pools are populous. The workforce may be younger. Birth

A younger workforce and higher levels of unemployment could indicate a labor pool that is ready to be tapped.

rates, along with infant mortality rates, are usually higher, especially in rural areas. Access to healthcare and education is limited for segments of the population. There may be inequalities as well. A small upper class might control much of the wealth. A larger, poorer portion does not have as many resources.

Unreliable infrastructure can lead to disruptions for companies that depend on continuous operations to survive and function. Safety is often at play too. Businesses are hesitant to establish themselves in a place where they—or their personnel—could face security risks. Given these factors it may seem that business investors face significant disadvantages with developing countries.

Those drawbacks aside, let us consider the positives, which in some cases can carry substantial weight. For instance, workers expect lower wages, as their daily living expenses cost less than those in developed nations. This can be beneficial for companies that need unskilled or skilled workers. A younger workforce and higher levels of unemployment could indicate a labor pool that is ready to be tapped. Economies that have not yet reached their potential could present an immense opportunity. If business goes well, the growth experienced might be quick and fast. It could surpass the rates of developed nations.

Choosing a Location

Due to the expenses related to producing goods and services in developed countries, businesses have long looked for places to shift part, or all, of their operations. Globalization trends began and picked up speed during the last century. Beginning in the 1970s, manufacturers started hiring outside firms to manage their less-than-essential processes. Soon firms were outsourcing 70 percent to 80 percent of their finished products. Large companies began handing off their IT operations. Sometimes they outsourced up to half of these tasks.[12]

To restructure their business model, companies evaluated their competitive advantages. They held on to their core competencies. Then they sought ways to outsource the remaining activities. Microsoft, for instance, may at one point have had the core competences of product design, product development, and marketing. All other nonessential tasks could be carried out by a different provider.[13]

A CLOSER LOOK AT OUTSOURCING

When a cost analysis is carried out, it can become evident why so many companies opt to hand off part or most of their operations. The expense reductions can vary. However, it is estimated that on average a firm could save 20 percent to 30 percent by outsourcing noncore business processes. These might include billing and payments, recruitment, back office work, and lead generation.[14]

The difference between wages in a developed country and a developing nation could lead to substantial cost reductions. British Airways reported that sending one thousand jobs to India resulted in a $23 million savings for the airline. A programmer in the US might earn $100,000 a year. That same position in a developing country might require a salary of between $25,000 and $35,000. (While at first glance there may appear to be a large discrepancy between $100,000 and $25,000 to $35,000, the lower salary coincides with the aforementioned lower costs of living in these nations.) In this way the

---

12   Michael F. Corbett, *The Outsourcing Revolution* (Chicago: Dearborn, 2004).

13   Corbett, *Outsourcing Revolution*.

14   ROI Solutions, "How Does Outsourcing Save Money?" accessed August 19, 2022, https://roicallcentersolutions.com/blog/how-does-outsourcing-save-money/.

company could reduce its labor costs for programmers by 70 percent to 90 percent through outsourcing.[15]

These savings can be passed on to consumers. Shoppers can purchase quality products for a lower cost. Companies report seeing hikes in productivity and competitiveness as well. Organizations can experience growth and increase performance by keeping their core functions in house and outsourcing the rest.

Of course the solution doesn't always run smoothly. When operating in other areas of the world, firms may come across a variety of challenges. Some of the common ones include

- Cultural and time zone clashes: When sending processes to different regions, it can be hard to communicate if neither party speaks the other's language. Working hours may also present issues, especially when outsourcing to areas on the other side of the globe. A factory in China might operate while executives in the US are sleeping. This lack of real-time communication causes delays and could lead to reduced productivity.

- Resistance from the home country: Citizens and other groups may protest when they see jobs being sent to a different area—and out of their reach. This can lead to tensions and put a damper on the reputation of a brand.

- Increased vulnerabilities: When outsourcing certain processes to a different country, companies are putting themselves at risk. A natural disaster can wreak havoc, especially in states that aren't prepared and don't have strong infrastructure and government support. If an earthquake or

---

15   Corbett, *Outsourcing Revolution*.

hurricane strikes, it could damage production plants. This could cause output levels to drop.

Whether these challenges impact a company's performance largely depends on several factors. These include the industry in which it operates, the locations it chooses, and the partnership it forms with the provider in the developing country. Moreover digital advances have helped improve communication and interaction between companies and their outsourced facilities. Today's workforce is increasingly more globally aware. Technologies like the internet provide connectivity and can reduce certain cultural barriers.

NEARSHORING POSSIBILITIES

As companies consider where to outsource, some see mitigated risks if operations are closer to home. The concept of nearshoring refers to transferring a business function to a nearby nation, as opposed to a country that is farther away. The idea is to stay within the same region.

For instance a firm in the Netherlands might opt to outsource some of its IT processes to a company in Poland. The two are geographically close and in the same time zone. This could make it easier to communicate during business hours. There may be more cultural similarities between the Netherlands and Poland than between the Netherlands and a farther-off country such as India. The corporation in the Netherlands might be more familiar with the safety precautions that need to be taken when traveling in Poland (if there are any that are different compared to the Netherlands).

The pandemic caused many supply chain interruptions throughout the globe. As a result some companies with outsourced operations in faraway countries experienced production interruptions. This was due, in large part, to factory shutdowns and shipping delays. The effect of Covid-19 raised questions among many about the possibilities of nearshoring. Staying closer to home, they pointed out, could reduce shipping times. It would make it easier to pivot to the market's changing demands.

Honduras: An Example of a Region with Potential

We've taken a tour around the world and considered some of the pros and cons that come from doing business in different countries and outsourcing. GK operates on a global level, with operations spanning from Pakistan to Mexico and beyond. As such, we recognize there are no right and wrong answers when choosing a country in which to operate.

Still it is valuable to consider what is best for a particular business segment and niche. In the case of GK, a thorough investigation of Honduras led to the conclusion that the country was ripe and ready for investment. Specifically there were geographical advantages, pathways for savings, and a workforce in waiting. Let's look at each of these.

EASY ACCESS

Honduras is nestled in the middle of Central America, with Nicaragua bordering it on the south and Guatemala on the north. It has four ports, creating access to both the Pacific and Atlantic oceans. Its road network connects the main cities of San Pedro Sula, Tegucigalpa, and Choloma, among others. Geographically Honduras is in close proximity to the US, the largest market in the world and its main trading partner. Daily direct flights run from its main cities to major hubs in the US.

PATHWAYS FOR SAVINGS

Honduras provides generous tax benefits. These facilitate operations for companies that want to invest in the country. The 2010 Investment Incentive and Protection Law created tax exemptions for firms that meet certain requirements. The Free Zone law established locations where organizations can receive exemptions on customs and other charges associated with bringing goods into those areas.

GK was far from the first company to see opportunity in Honduras. The country has long exported coffee, agricultural products, and seafood, including shrimp and lobster. During the early 1900s, American corporations invested in banana production in the northern portion of the country. Its manufacturing sector began in 1976.[16] Though it was small during the initial years, contributing to just 15 percent of the total GDP in 1992, it found its niche in textile products, largely sent to the US.[17]

WORKFORCE IN WAITING

During the height of its banana trade during the last century, two multinational corporations, Chiquita Brands International and Dole Food Company, had an extensive reach in Honduras. These companies established sites that could accommodate workers from Honduras and executives from the US. Some of their investments led to bilingual schools. There the children learned both English and Spanish. This caused an influence of the English language among children and employees associated with the banana companies.

---

16   Asociación Hondureña de Maquiladoras, "The Manufacturing Industry in Honduras," accessed August 19, 2022, http://www.ahm-honduras.com/?page_id=1843.

17   Photius, "Honduras Manufacturing," revised November 10, 2004, https://photius. com/countries/honduras/economy/honduras_economy_manufacturing.html.

The bilingual system remains attractive for private schools throughout the country. Due to the history of interaction with the banana companies, citizens have a heritage of English. They can speak it in a clear, highly articulated manner. This trait creates an up-and-coming workforce prepared to participate in the international scene. In addition, 60 percent of Honduran professionals and business executives speak English.[18]

Honduras has a young population, with an average age of just over twenty-four years old.[19] Many are looking for an opportunity, a chance to get ahead in life. If they don't find the career paths they are looking for in Honduras, they may set their sights on other places. They could consider migrating. On the other hand, if there are environments laid out where they can grow personally and professionally, they might be inclined to stay.

It is with these thoughts that GK turned to Honduras. In 1991 it came to join the small manufacturing sector specializing in textile and yarn. During the coming years, it would expand and continue to build, eventually reaching beyond the borders of Honduras and branching into other industries. Now, when people ask us at GK about Honduras, we have more than just a dream and vision to share. We have results, which we'll look at more in depth in the next chapters.

I like to point out one nugget of information during conversations about investing in Honduras. I say that investing in Honduras is similar to how we invest in our valued relationships. We make a

18   I Love Languages, "What Languages Do They Speak in Honduras?" accessed August 19, 2022, https://www.ilovelanguages.com/what-language-is-spoken-in-honduras/.

19   Knoema, "Honduras Median Age of Population, 1950-2021," accessed August 19, 2022, https://knoema.com/atlas/Honduras/topics/Demographics/Age/Median-age-of-population.

commitment. We spend time and energy growing the relationship. We look for ways to improve and make memories together.

After all, investing in Honduras involves a commitment to its people. When jobs are created, lives are impacted. It took time and effort to get established. Making profits required significant dedication to processes and attention to costs. We worked hard for many years to make the company and country better.

When GK first established itself in Honduras, many questions remained unanswered. What would the future bring? Would it be possible to make an impact? Could GK be a leader in sustainable growth?—the face of corporate responsibility?

> *Making profits required significant dedication to processes and attention to costs.*

At the time I didn't have all the answers. That said, I was convinced I had spotted an opportunity. There was a growing demand in nearshoring from the US. I noticed tax incentives that would help the bottom line. I spotted a labor pool that was ready to work and learn. Even as others shied away, I invested long term into the country.

And I'm glad I did. As it turns out, Honduras was ripe with potential. As you evaluate countries where you want to establish operations, think through your priorities. Do you need a skilled labor force? How do costs play into your decision? What type of land or facilities will work in your business plan? As you answer these questions, keep in mind the power of potential. Countries that are set up to scale could create immense opportunities for your own company.

HOW TO DO BUSINESS IN DEVELOPING COUNTRIES

- When exploring the map, keep geography in mind. Do you need to have operations in a specific region? Is it important to have access to certain markets?

- If others steer away from a certain country, ask them why. Be sure to investigate it yourself too. You might find commonly overlooked features that could give you a competitive advantage. Perhaps properties are priced low, workers are anxious to learn, or local governments want to promote your industry.

- Be on the lookout for ways that your company and the country of operations could scale together. If the economy is set to take off, align your business plan so you can both achieve exponential growth.

- Tax incentives can go a long way for the bottom line. If a country has recently implemented trade laws, find out what they are. Lean into favorable conditions.

CHAPTER 3

Make Sustainability Part of the Business Plan

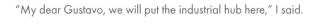

"My dear Gustavo, we will put the industrial hub here," I said.

I stood next to Gustavo Raudales, CEO of GK Real Estate. We were surveying a plot of land in rural Honduras, about thirty kilometers outside of San Pedro Sula. At that moment there was no industry in sight.

In fact our gaze fell on a very different view, one that was far from a manufacturing zone. We were looking at a pasture. A cow lowed in the background, then continued chewing on grass.

"You want an industrial hub here, I understand," Gustavo began. "There's just one thing."

"Yes?" I knew Gustavo well and valued his insight. As the leader of GK's real estate division, he had a long track record of overseeing its trajectory and finishing successful projects. He accompanied me on this surveillance trip as I shared my vision for the next step in the GK business. The company had started manufacturing in the area with a focus on textiles and yarn spinning. Now it was time to expand and create an industrial hub.

"All I see are cows," Gustavo said.

He was right, of course. The lovely green valley served as a pastureland for cattle.

Would GK put up an industrial hub and take away this beautiful scenery? Would it come in and destroy the animals, the land, and the surrounding nature?

If it did, it wouldn't be living up to its goals. As such, my vision was far from demolition. It encompassed developing, regenerating, and giving life.

"We will keep it green," I assured Gustavo.

Fast-forward to today. Visitors who enter the industrial hub that now operates where Gustavo and I once stood are greeted with a panorama that is largely the same.

Indeed I will attest that GK has worked to keep the center eco-friendly and sustainable. The effort is ongoing, which is part of the thrill of corporate responsibility. How do we take a place and transform it into a space that businesses can use? How do we simultaneously contribute to the environment?

To keep the vision aligned with our goals, GK named the industrial hub "Green Valley." I invite you now to observe as I guide you through what this center offers. We'll begin by discussing some of the main industries that operate in the hub. We'll also look at its growth and renewable energy projects. We'll explore the nursery, which oversees its conservation and replanting efforts. We'll take an overview of the sustainable housing provided to improve the lives of its workers and encourage them to remain in Honduras.

As you read consider your own sustainable initiatives. Are there ways you can be creative, as GK was? Do you see opportunities to start green practices within your operations? When investing in a different country, you won't want to overlook the environment. Ask what's being done to reduce waste. If you don't find an answer that satisfies, create a green example that others can follow.

Streamlining for Efficiency

Green Valley is a home away from home for US publicly listed corporations and Fortune 500 companies. It hosts manufacturers from around the world, including Europe and North Africa multinational organizations. It contains the largest textile and automotive wire harness industrial clusters in Central America.

Investors are often drawn to Green Valley because it provides turnkey solutions. When companies decide to set up operations within the hub, they can receive ready-to-use facilities and services. There's no need for them to visit the place, design their plant, and find a construction company to build it. They don't have to hire an attorney to fill out the legal paperwork required for them to operate. Firms can avoid flying down a management team to find and hire all their workers.

GK provides customized services for investors' core and ancillary needs. These cover all steps, ranging from start-up to running operations. Offerings include business registration, permits, talent acquisition, employee training, expat relocation, supervision of specialized installations, and 24-7 support.

As we mentioned in the previous chapter, companies that decide to outsource are often motivated by cost reductions. If they manage all the setup, hiring, and daily operations of a facility, those savings can quickly evaporate. They may find they aren't familiar with how business dealings are carried out in a foreign-to-them place, they might not speak the language, and they could be unaware of how to find reliable local suppliers. With GK's system, those risks are mitigated, which enables investors to save on management expenses.

Speed is another essential component for companies with outsourcing needs. Given this, GK set up processes to expedite start-up projects. For instance consider the following cases that reflect common requirements for companies operating in the manufacturing hub. They list the amount of time GK uses to have operations ready compared to the industry average:

Establish a wire harness operation for three thousand employees: GK's start-up time is eight to ten months; the industry average is twelve to eighteen months.

Create a textile mill for fabric production with an output of three million pounds per week: GK's start-up time is twelve months; industry average is eighteen months.

Develop production infrastructure for wires and cables (six cable extrusion lines): GK's start-up time is seven to nine months; industry average is twelve to fourteen months.

Set up an airbag connector plant: GK's start-up time is six months; industry average is ten months.

Green Initiatives

True to its name, Green Valley today boasts lovely greenery and landscaped boulevards. This scenery is readily visible as guests move throughout the hub. The properties of the companies inside the hub are adorned with carefully placed plants.

An onsite, full-time gardener oversees the maintenance and upkeep of the various species. A full nursery is located within the hub, where plants are grown and then distributed both within Green Valley and to nearby communities. An intricate compost and watering system completes the full plant life-cycle. The entire operation is self-sustaining.

When the hub was built, several of the native trees to the area were not cut down. Instead workers created signs that identify the species and placed them near the plants. Now workers and visitors can appreciate the displays as they pass by.

A pond amid the hub provides a retreat. Stocked with fish, it is also a food source. Workers frequently bring a fishing rod with them when they enter Green Valley. They stop at the pond before or after their shift. They can catch a meal of fish at their leisure.

This manufacturing hub lives out the sustainability mindset in other areas as well. It has infrastructure that can operate independently for its electricity, water, and telecommunications needs. Its solar panels portray a renewable energy project. It has aggressive programs for waste management and water treatment, including a full gray water recycling system.

At Green Valley, structures are ISO 14001:2015 certified. This standard lays out requirements for an environmental management system that an organization can use to enhance its eco-related performance. It contributes to the following sustainable development goals, as adopted by the UN: no poverty; zero hunger; good health and well-being; quality education; clean water and sanitation; affordable and clean energy; decent work and economic growth; industry, innovation, and infrastructure; responsible consumption and production; climate action; life below water; and life on land.[20]

---

20   ISO, "ISO 14001:2015: Environmental Management Systems—Requirements with Guidance for Use," accessed August 19, 2022, https://www.iso.org/standard/60857.html.

GK has also received the Living Future Challenge certification, which is a rigorous building design standard. Its framework consists of seven petals, and each one represents a performance area:

- Energy: Relying only on solar power.

- Water: Creating developments that operate within the water balance of a given place and climate.

- Place: Restoring a healthy interrelationship with nature.

- Materials: Endorsing products that are safe for all species throughout their life-cycle.

- Equity: Supporting justice in the world.

- Beauty: Celebrating design in a way that uplifts the human spirit.

- Health and Happiness: Creating environments that optimize well-being.[21]

The TRUE certification program rates how facilities are managing their resources. It measures their methods to minimize nonhazardous, solid wastes and maximize their use of resources. Overall it helps facilities on their pathway toward zero waste.[22] Green Valley is in the process of obtaining the TRUE certification that includes zero waste and LEED (which stands for Leadership in Energy and Environmental Design—more on this in chapter 4).

---

21   International Living Future Institute, "Living Building Challenge Basics," accessed August 19, 2022, https://living-future.org/lbc/basics4-0/.

22   TRUE, "Less Waste, Higher Efficiency, Greater Savings," accessed August 19, 2022, https://true.gbci.org/.

GK's decarbonization path at Green Valley includes a five-year program to achieve carbon neutrality. This involves the use of renewable energy, which is currently in operation and is expanding. It is the largest industrial plant of its kind in the region. It also carries out reforestation, cogeneration, and solid waste management programs.

Staying at Home

When workers take on a job at Green Valley, they may be upleveling their income and lifestyle in a significant way. With a manufacturing job, they receive access to free onsite medical care for their needs. They also gain the security of a steady paycheck, which may not have been an option for them in the past.

Many of the job positions require unskilled or low-skilled labor. As such, most of the employees at Green Valley have not completed a high school education. If they didn't have a job with GK, they could be carrying out subsistence living. They might be making food and selling it on the street to try and make ends meet. These jobs, however, don't provide the same level of continuity that a manufacturing job offers.

If employees didn't have a job with GK, they could be carrying out subsistence living.

In addition, through a housing program in which GK and the government participate, workers have the opportunity to purchase and own a home. One of these houses, catered to moderate income levels, may be the first modern house an employee lives in. Located just outside of Green Valley, these residential areas make it easy to walk or bike to work in a safe environment.

Building Green Valley would not be the end of GK's projects in Honduras or elsewhere. As we'll see in the following chapters, the company has extensions in other countries in Central America, Mexico, the US, and Pakistan. In every place the mission to be the face of corporate responsibility, ranging from sustainable solutions to improving everyday lives, remains.

The business model is designed to confront—and reverse—one of the main challenges the workforces in Honduras and other Central American countries face. When they don't have the chance to learn skills and get a job in their own home country, there is an urge to go find a place where they can better their livelihoods. Most of the migrants from Central America that head to the US come from El Salvador, Guatemala, and Honduras. Collectively these entities are called the Northern Triangle, due to their geographic position in the upper end of the region. Guatemala borders Mexico. Travelers cross the country en route to Mexico's northern neighbor.

In Central America GK's business ventures keep an average of sixty thousand direct and indirect workers at home. These employees stay, rather than migrating in pursuit of job opportunities in other lands. For every five thousand new jobs that are added locally through GK's model, an additional fifteen thousand Hondurans will choose to remain home. This multiplying factor holds true in other countries of the Northern Triangle. For every five thousand positions in Guatemala, seventeen thousand will opt not to migrate; in El Salvador, a surplus of five thousand jobs leads to persuading ten thousand individuals to remain within its borders.

There is evidence that some of these efforts have been making a difference. Workers that come to Green Valley are more likely to stay at the center, rather than look for a different job. From January to July 2021, the average attrition in Green Valley stood below 1.5 percent each month. According to reports from companies operating in Honduras, the average dropout rate in competing manufacturing centers in Honduras averages between 5 percent and 7 percent every month. The yearly attrition rate for a wire harness manufacturer in Green Valley is less than 3 percent. This same company has facilities in a different hub in Mexico, where it has annual fallout rates that are higher than 10 percent.

When they stay, they often do so for the long term. At Green Valley, 45 percent of the employees have worked for their companies for three or more years. These positions serve, in a real sense, to anchor them. They can stay home, provide for their families, and be involved in their communities.

I still recall standing with Gustavo, looking over the field that eventually turned into Green Valley. When I move through it today, I see workers who are putting in a shift and then leaving to spend time with their loved ones. I am glad we made the decision to build.

The cows found a new home. International companies discovered a place where they could operate. Employees get a new and improved life—one paycheck, one year, and one residence at a time.

HOW TO DO BUSINESS IN DEVELOPING COUNTRIES

Green Valley is home to Fortune 500 companies, industry leaders, and multinational firms from the US, Europe, and North Africa.

- The hub's commitment to sustainability has helped to protect the environment in the area while simultaneously giving the companies it hosts access to eco benefits.

- Workers who take a job at Green Valley are more likely to stay with the company. Their position provides an elevation in lifestyle and encourages them to remain in the country, rather than migrating illegally to Mexico and the US.

- When doing business, find the average wage offered to employees in a specific country. Consider offering a salary that is slightly above local expectations. Creating a comfortable lifestyle for workers can increase retention rates.

CHAPTER 4

Create Your Own Paradise

I vividly remember a conversation I had with a close friend of mine on a construction site. GK was in the process of building a segment of Altia Smart City, a pioneering ecosystem, in San Pedro Sula. I had envisioned a place that would be powered by solar energy. It would be a technology hub in Central America. The hub would serve as a solution for international companies with BPO and ITO outsourcing needs. GK would help provide local workers for these firms. This would give Hondurans in the area the chance to better their economic lives.

In that memorable instant—which is forever etched in my mind—when I stood with my friend on the grounds that would bear the name Altia Smart City, everything was stalled out. It wasn't that GK's vision was off or that a problem in the blueprints had come up.

A different, larger problem was before us.

It was one that I had neither instigated nor participated in. It was a countrywide issue. I, living in a land that wasn't my birth country, was feeling its impact. Moreover it was affecting GK—and every other business and person in Honduras.

The year was 2009. A coup had taken place, during which the military had escorted the president out of the country over political disagreements. The international community had responded by with-drawing sources of aid and reducing trade.

Unrest had loomed before the event. After the incident the horizon was full of uncertainty. News related to the event saturated global headlines. Via the internet and television, international figures shared their opinions about what should be done.

Meanwhile, in Honduras, I stood upon a dream. I surveyed the Altia site. I didn't know if the crashed economy would ever return.

And next to me stood my friend.

"How many stories high is that building?" he asked, looking up at one of Altia's towers.

"Fifteen," I replied. The space was designed to provide outsourc-ing services to international companies. These firms could rent the units. GK would oversee the business structuring, interior custom-izations, and legal requirements. The firms could simply arrive and start operations.

Now, with his gaze fixed on the building, my companion asked another question. "How many of those are filled or slotted to be filled?"

"None," I replied.

A low sigh came out of his mouth. We stood, side by side, gazing up at that building. Time passed.

What will happen next? we both silently wondered.

The building stood just as mute. While protests abounded throughout the country, and the political situation showed no signs of smoothing over, Altia remained. Quietly. Waiting. I did too.

"Are you going to finish building this place?" my dear confidant asked next. His gaze drifted to the rest of the site. He knew my plans, my hopes of building this ecosystem that would break barriers in nearly every sense. It would be a leader in sustainability, provide a boost for the local economy, slow down immigration, and provide a top-notch solution for Fortune 500 companies. In short it would represent nearly everything we at GK could think of, packaged in one.

It was a good question. Surely others were pondering the same inquiry.

I responded with my heart—a simple "Yes."

Again, another low sigh from my friend. Then he put his arm around me.

"I know you well, and you know me," he began. "There are two things about this project I can share with you."

"Yes?" I waited for his explanation.

"First, my company doesn't have the resources to build this kind of a project," he began.

Fair point, I thought. If his organization was like the others throughout Honduras, it was feeling the hit of the economic and political distress. We all were to some degree.

"Second, if I did have the funds to put up this building, I wouldn't now have the legs to look up at it," he concluded.

Also fair, I mused.

What was to be done? I knew, intuitively, that I would go forward. The coup, while distressing, wasn't the first obstacle GK had faced. I knew it wouldn't be the last. The key was to keep making progress, as we were able.

Now, more than ten years later, as I look back on that story and recall our shared words, the memory still brings a smile to my face. The expression doesn't stem from a sentiment of resentment or an urge to share the outcome of GK's Altia initiative. Instead it is one of gratitude, a pleasant recognition that despite the challenges that come with being in a developing country, there is plenty of opportunity—and benefits for everyone who gets involved and works toward a common goal.

To get a full understanding of how GK began Altia and its relationship with the people in Honduras, it can be worthwhile to step back in time and linger with me during the early phases of this smart city. We'll take a deeper look at the crisis that hit Honduras and other countries in 2008 and 2009 and the political instability during that time. We'll consider how those spaces in the building were filled (trust me—it was not easy!) and look at how Altia developed over the years. Finally we'll spend some time evaluating a critical ongoing issue in Honduras—that is, deployed migrants—and review how that challenge is interwoven into the story of Honduras and the coup. We'll conclude by looking at how Altia welcomes migrants who leave the country and then return home.

Financial Crisis and More

When people say to me, "It must not be easy to run a company in a developing country," I agree with them—to a certain extent. Certainly there are obstacles to face. A main one consists of the political infrastructure. Perhaps the example of the Honduras coup that took place in 2009 can help us appreciate what everyday business dealings are like when stability—that often-longed-for characteristic—is wiped away.

The tale of political woes in Honduras begins much earlier than 2009. In fact the coup that year was hardly a first for the country. The pages of its history books are filled with tales of military governments, political interventions, human rights abuses, and skirmishes with other countries.

Going back several centuries, the explorer Christopher Columbus set foot in Honduras in 1502. At the time, he met with the indigenous people living there. A little more than twenty years later, Spain started its conquest of the region, eventually taking over and governing it until 1821. That year Honduras shook off Spain's control and went on to become part of Mexico. It gained its independence in 1840. Military governments controlled the country for the next decades.[23]

A couple of notable coups occurred during the 1900s. In 1963 Colonel Osvaldo Lopez Arellano took power after leading a revolt. General Policarpo Paz Garcia overthrew the head of government in 1978. During that century Honduras also went to war with El Salvador, suffered through human rights violations by armed forces and right-wing death squads, and battled street gangs and organized crime.

Certainly this overview doesn't do justice to the detailed and full account of the country's past. Indeed entire texts have been written in an attempt to explain the past of Honduras and how its interactions with other countries, its geographical setting, and its resources have all played a role in its political setting. Our brief listing also overlooks several positive highlights on the country's past, including its democratic transition that began in 1980. That year elections were held for an assembly that produced the country's current constitution. Voters have cast ballots for the president, legislators, and municipal governments since 1981. Beginning in 1994 Honduras has had an attorney general lead a semiautonomous public ministry as well. This public ministry heads most public prosecutions, including corruption and organized crime.[24]

I believe it's worth including this history in its brevity, as it helps us paint the picture of what Honduras is like as a country. We can see that when GK began constructing Altia, it did not break ground on a site surrounded by a developed country with a stable govern-

---

23 BBC, "Honduras Profile—Timeline," May 6, 2018, https://www.bbc.com/news/world-latin-america-18974519.

24 US Embassy in Honduras, "U.S. Embassy in Honduras: Political Section," accessed August 17, 2022, https://hn.usembassy.gov/embassy/tegucigalpa/sections-offices/political-section/.

ment. (We haven't even mentioned the economy yet! But I will in a moment.) Rather it was operating in a country that has a past filled with conflict. These incidents have consequences. While we can point out that people—including families and children—often suffer the most during hard times, it is also true that businesses frequently face specific barriers when political hardships occur. When companies suffer, it often impacts families directly or indirectly, through the loss of jobs and economic support. That's precisely what happened to many companies and households in Honduras around the time of the coup in 2009.

2008-2009 CRISIS

The financial crisis that hit the world's economy in 2008 further aggravated the challenges rippling through Honduras. With a poverty rate of more than 60 percent, traditional struggles to survive were amplified. Unemployment levels grew as companies closed their doors, either temporarily or permanently.[25]

Tough labor conditions often lead to health challenges, and Honduras is no exception. Around the time of the world economic crisis, the country was dealing with an infant mortality level of thirty-one per thousand. Chronic malnutrition afflicted approximately one-third of children as well.[26]

President Manuel Zelaya came to power in 2006 in Honduras and targeted reforms for the poor. However, some of his actions, including an increase to the minimum wage and forming close ties

---

25   Council of Hemispheric Affairs, "Honduras: The Devastating Effects of the June 28th Coup on the Honduran Economy Are Not Likely to Be Undone by Illegitimate Elections," December 2, 2009, https://www.coha.org/honduras-the-devastating-effects-of-the-june-28th-coup-on-the-honduran-economy-are-not-likely-to-be-undone-by-illegitimate-elections/.

26   Council of Hemispheric Affairs, "Honduras: Devastating Effects."

with Venezuela's socialist president Hugo Chavez, stirred emotions.[27] President Zelaya then announced his plans to ask voters whether they supported convening a national constituent assembly to discuss amending the constitution, including a discussion on the conditions of presidential reelection.[28] Many feared a desire to rewrite the constitution to allow for his own reelection.

As a result of these occurrences, on June 28, 2009, a group of soldiers surrounded Zelaya's residence before dawn, disarmed his security guards, and forced him into exile.[29] Roberto Micheletti, the president of congress at the time and the next in line for president, became the interim president. In response to the unrest, the UN, the Organization of American States, and the European Union denounced the military coup. The US withdrew military aid and canceled diplomatic visas to important figures in the interim government.[30]

The exact causes and accusations surrounding the coup are beyond the scope of this book's discussion. As such, it is sufficient to say that a new president, Porfirio Lobo, was elected and assumed power after seven months of domestic political crisis. On January 27, 2010, he was inaugurated and led the country for the next four years.[31]

---

27   Helen Popper, "Honduras Coup Tensions Take Toll on Economy," Reuters, November 20, 2009, https://www.reuters.com/article/us-honduras-economy-idUK-TRE5AJ47320091120.

28   Physicians for Human Rights, "Honduras: Constitutional Crisis and Coup D'Etat (2009)," accessed August 17, 2022, https://phr.org/honduras-constitutional-crisis-and-coup/.

29   Associated Press, "Honduras President Arrested in Military Coup," The Guardian, June 28, 2009, https://www.theguardian.com/world/2009/jun/28/honduras-coup-president-zelaya.

30   Mica Rosenberg, "Honduras Leader Firm against World Pressure," Reuters, August 1, 2009, https://www.reuters.com/article/us-honduras-micheletti-idUS-TRE5700BB20090801.

31   Defense Technical Information Center, "Honduras-U.S. Relations," accessed August 17, 2022, https://apps.dtic.mil/sti/citations/ADA514802.

Let's circle back to that point in time surrounding the coup and look at it from the perspective of everyday life for Hondurans and businesses. The ousting of President Zelaya plunged the country into turmoil, costing it $50 million a day for the next five months, with much of the burden falling on the poor. In 2008 Honduras exported over $4 billion worth of goods to the US, its main trade partner, and received imports of around $2.5 billion. Exports in 2009 to the US plunged by $1 billion.[32] Clearly these were rough periods for everyone, from the fruit seller on the streets of a village to midsize factories and international firms like GK.

A Reason to Invest

Perhaps my close friend was thinking of the country's history and instability during our conversation about GK's empty tower in Altia. Maybe he was concerned that international companies would be hesitant to invest in a place that was going through turmoil. He likely knew that countries such as the US were pulling out aid, and trade was dropping. We all were aware that the economy was going through a dire stretch.

One of the main purposes of Altia, as I mentioned earlier, was to become a technology and business processing outsourcing hub in Central America. Specifically GK had spotted a gap in the area of business process outsourcing (BPO). This segment involves a company sending one or more of its IT-intensive business procedures to a provider, in this case GK's Altia tenants. In turn Altia tenants would oversee the administration and management of these services,

---

32   Council of Hemispheric Affairs, "Honduras: Devastating Effects."

based on measurable performance metrics.[33] Altia was designed to offer services such as call centers, data centers, back-office services, telemarketing, and information technologies.

The potential was there, built in a complex that promoted a safe, easy-to-use working environment for international clients. Given the rise in technology use throughout the globe, the need for BPO was growing. Altia could provide a nearshore solution that catered to each tech-related process a company might have.

There was one issue that had to be sorted through, of course. Due to the coup and political unrest, Honduras faced an uphill battle in terms of attracting investments and international companies. Indeed other industries crashed when President Zelaya was ejected from the country. Tourism had been in decline during the months leading up to the ousting. Governments warned travelers against heading to Honduras due to the brewing political situation there. After the coup tourism plummeted by 80 percent. Some of the most popular destinations in the country, including the beaches on the north coast along the Caribbean, sat nearly vacant. The same held true for the archeological park of Copán Ruins.[34] Travel was down, imports and exports were in a slump … How would the other industries fare?

Perhaps the segment GK was most concerned about, in relation to its Altia operations, was BPO and call-center services. What would the reaction of the international community be to a country that seemed to attract negative media coverage? Would anyone want to invest in it or start business operations there?

---

33   Gartner Glossary, "Business Process Outsourcing," accessed August 17, 2022, https://www.gartner.com/en/information-technology/glossary/business-process-outsourcing-bpo#:~:text=Business%20process%20outsourcing%20(BPO)%20is,defined%20and%20measurable%20performance%20metrics.

34   Tourism Master, "Tourism in Times of Political Crisis: The Case of Honduras," accessed August 17, 2022, http://www.tourism-master.com/2009/10/04/tourism-in-times-of-political-crisis-the-case-of-honduras/.

In the short term, it appeared that the answer to this last question was a resounding "no." At least that's what I heard time and again when I went to visit companies in other countries. I could understand their point of view. I, who had lived in the country for nearly twenty years by then, had a much different view of Honduras than others, especially those who had never set foot in its borders or started company operations there.

There was a scenario that played out so many times it became familiar to me. It occurred when I met with executives. I might be invited to the C-suite office to share some of Altia's features with a company that was interested in learning more and considering outsourcing some of its IT needs. I would show up to the meeting, ready to discuss the arrangements GK makes to provide convenience at every step. I had presentations and a brochure lined up and could readily answer whatever question was directed toward me.

I could practically sense the brochure I had left with them being tossed into the garbage bin.

I would begin with the presentation tailored to the company and show areas where Altia could provide assistance. I would outline cost savings through outsourcing and include information on the ready-to-use facilities. Then I would hand out a brochure that depicted the locations and the features I had mentioned.

At this point the question would come up. An executive, maybe the CEO, would lean over and ask, "Who else is there?"

What could I say? They wanted to know what other businesses were already operating in Altia. They were looking for confirmation that it was safe to go there as well.

I had to answer in truth. So I openly responded, "Nobody."

54

That usually ended the discussion.

As I walked out of the door, on my way to exiting the meeting and building, I could practically sense the brochure I had left with them being tossed into the garbage bin.

I hardly blame those executives. To hear of a foreign place that just had a coup or was full of political unrest and be promised stable, smoothly running services there? It just didn't seem possible.

Ultimately Altia

In addition to finding clients, GK had to educate potential workers about the role they would play. At the time, BPO was an unknown industry in Honduras. Given this, community members lacked an awareness of the benefits a hub could bring. Local authorities were hesitant to offer support for unfamiliar services.

To overcome these challenges, at GK we worked to share the BPO story with others. We related the advantages it could bring a place like Honduras. We trained workers to give them the skills they needed.

One step at a time, and one client at a time, the places in Altia in San Pedro Sula filled. Workers were hired, processes established, and operations started. In time, as mentioned, the political environment found even ground, and the economy leveled.

During this stage a new pattern began. It consisted of one company, after getting settled in Altia, recommending the place to another organization. This second firm, in turn, would decide to outsource to Honduras, often directly to Altia. Again once operations had been established, the second corporation frequently sent out recommendations to another. The rhythm continued with referrals generating new leads and creating more jobs in the area.

What, exactly, did clients find once they had contacted Altia and asked for a tour? Let's have a look.

"ALWAYS ON" CONTINUITY

It's essential in certain business operations, especially those that are technology driven, that utility systems do not fail or break down. Any pause in continuity could lead to extended delays later or a hefty loss due to the downtime caused. To avoid this Altia is fully independent from the local electricity, water, and telecommunications infrastructure. In other words it can run on its own. Like Green Valley it is designed to assure investors can rely on utilities.

GK set up Altia to be independent from government involvement. Like our other endeavors, the hub is self-sustaining. It produces its own energy and doesn't rely on large political contributions or contracts. In this way it avoids risks related to fragile political structures. GK can make ethical choices and steer away from corruption-related events.

HIGHEST GREEN INTERNATIONAL STANDARDS

Similar to the efforts in Green Valley, Altia is based on the concept of renewable resources and has a rooftop solar energy power system. It is on track to reduce its CO_2 emissions by 60 percent by 2026. In every initiative it takes on, it seeks to comply with the highest international standards for sustainability.

The buildings at Altia are LEED designed. When investors use LEED-certified buildings, it can help them meet their ESG goals. Systems can be set up to prioritize building efficiency, decrease operational costs, and promote productivity. A few of the cost benefits that come from LEED-designed buildings compared to other structures include the following:

- Use of 25 percent less energy

- Consumption of 11 percent less water

- Maintenance costs that are 20 percent lower

- A decrease of 10 percent in operation costs[35]

Implementing LEED can bring positive outcomes that stretch beyond direct financial results. It provides ample health benefits for workers:

- Improved indoor air quality

- More access to daylight

- An absence of chemicals found in paints and finishings[36]

These features have been found to reduce the number of absentee days workers take. For instance those with asthma, allergies, and other respiratory-related conditions frequently find it alleviating to work in LEED-designed structures. Employees with depression and stress may appreciate the extra light and be more productive.[37]

A HOLISTIC SOLUTION

Let's run the main features and components of Altia to give you an idea of what it is like to do business there.

Features

- State-of-the-art security system: As soon as you enter, you step inside a place that prioritizes safety. Altia has an app

---

35 Lisa Montgomery, "How LEED Certification Can Save Your Organization Money," My Tech Decisions, December 26, 2018, https://mytechdecisions.com/compliance/how-leed-certification-can-save-your-organization-money/.

36 U.S. Green Building Council, "Why LEED," accessed August 18, 2022, https://www.usgbc.org/leed/why-leed.

37 U.S. Green Building Council, "Why LEED."

that visitors can use. Once you're registered you can enter seamlessly through the entry protocol. The entire area is monitored around the clock and closed off, emphasizing security for all who enter and work there.

- Free zone for the BPO industry: The first of its kind in Honduras, the free zone grants investors exemption from local, national, and sales taxes. There is no expiration date for these free-zone tax benefits.

- Customized recruitment department: Altia has its own department to help attract talent. When investors come, Altia takes their specific needs for starting up and assists in the vetting and hiring of workers. Through growth periods, the recruitment department can be used again.

- Free counseling services: When employees or their families need psychological help, they can visit Altia's counseling center. There is no charge for the service, which is available at any time.

- Twenty-four seven in-house support team: If investors have an issue that needs attention, they can use the Altia ticketing system. This allows any problem to be addressed immediately, whether it be related to a legal matter, an operating issue, maintenance, or other task.

- An experienced staff: Team members have six sigma knowledge, CX certifications, and digital citizen continuous education.

Components

- Altia Business Park: This consists of four towers ranging from six to fifteen floors. Each of these is designed to cater to BPO and ITO companies.

- RecZen: Often companies that outsource need to build their own space where staff can take lunch breaks and relax. This is not the case in Altia. Instead, thanks to the RecZen, all investors who operate in the park have access to it for their workers. It is two levels high, plus it has a rooftop. On the first floor, employees find a full food-and-drink area, complete with a cafeteria, buffet, convenience store, coffee shop, and dining space. Employees who want to relax can head up to the second floor and rooftop area, which have attractive spaces for meeting and holding events.

- Altara: As the first lifestyle center in Honduras, this shopping complex is interconnected with the park. It features two levels that have entertainment such as movie theaters, retail stores, a gym, and a food court. It is open to the public and to Altia workers. Live events are frequently held in Altara, including music performances, fashion shows, seasonal festivals, and artisan markets. Workers at Altia have access to a bank there, and they receive special discounts at most stores and restaurants.

- Unitec: This university, which has more than 150 campuses in more than fifty countries, has a site that can be accessed by foot from Altia. This allows employees at Altia to work and study at the same place. Integrating this university component has enabled Altia to grow a highly qualified talent pool.

- Courtyard Hotel by Marriott: Where do investors and others who visit Altia stay? This hotel is designed to meet executive needs and streamline the business process. It encompasses the lifestyle concept, enabling guests to be within walking distance of shops, restaurants, and other facilities they can use as needed.

- Altia Residences: Where do staff members live? Through the construction of residences, they have a home right next to their workplace, making it easy to walk over for their shift.

In addition to a site in San Pedro Sula, Altia has a center in Tegucigalpa, the capital of Honduras. With a constant eye for sustainability, Altia is setting an example for others in Central America and around the world of how a smart technological city can run—and thrive.

A Chance to Grow

Working in the BPO and ITO services generally requires a higher skill level than manufacturing. Most of the employees at Altia are considered medium-skilled workers, meaning they have a high school education. Many are bilingual, speaking both English and Spanish fluently.

When hiring these workers, GK gives them opportunities that extend beyond a job and income. It offers vocational upskilling and language and remedial courses. For instance workers who do not have a high school diploma might take a job and then study at night to complete their degree.

The smart city design promotes the concept of a career and upward trajectory. Employees often attend the nearby Unitec. The university offers degrees in a variety of fields, including engineering, business, and medicine. It also gives customized education and training programs when investors have specific needs. Among Unitec graduates 40 percent go on to work for GK or investors at Altia. Some take on managerial roles. In this sense many employees find a long-term path that is not widely available in other areas of Honduras.

THE OPPORTUNITY TO STAY

Due to the extensive benefits offered through Altia, workers tend to remain there. Approximately 35 percent of workers have been with the company for at least three years. In addition, 9 percent have been with the company for longer than five years.

When proper incentives and potential pathways for personal and professional advancement are given, the risk for churn can be reduced. This has been evident at GK's Altia, as the attrition rate from 2017 to 2021 ranged from 6.5 percent to 13.91 percent each year. Compared to a similar BPO company with facilities in the US that has a turnover rate of 90 percent each year, these percentages are significantly lower.

Many also note that the working environment is a bit like paradise. For those raised in a country where more than half of the population lives at poverty level or below, the day-to-day scenery doesn't resemble a technology park. When they step inside, they are immersed in a LEED-designed environment. This clean environment often feels like a new world and an enlightening opportunity.

What's more, they don't just show up to work and then leave. These workers can take their breaks on site at the RecZen, head to the shopping center, and exercise—all in one place. This integrated approach embraces the live-work lifestyle and paves the way for a future generation of Honduras—one that is interested in staying at the same job and moving up.

A WELCOMING HOME

When individuals or families leave Honduras and head north in search of a different job, they can run into challenges. These obstacles occur at the border—and upon their return to their native country. Those that are deported often face myriad problems when they try to integrate back into the communities they left in Honduras and find employment again. They might be out of money or reimmersed into a difficult situation. This tough setting could have originally motivated them to leave.

GK doesn't reject potential employees if they have a deportation notification come up during the background check. Altia, in fact, has a track record of hiring a substantial number of Hondurans who are returning after being deported from the US. At one company within Altia, returnees account for approximately 30 percent of the Honduran workforce.

Looking back I am glad GK built the first tower for Altia and thankful that operations continued. I still talk to my friend about our conversation on that dreary day during the year of the coup. He knows, like me, that had we not persevered, more of the workforce in Honduras could have been lost to migration. Instead we now have operating towers and a loyal employee base. Moreover we have created longstanding partnerships with world-renowned companies that use our spaces every day—and love them.

BUSINESS OPPORTUNITIES IN DEVELOPING COUNTRIES

- Altia is a pioneering sustainable ecosystem designed to provide BPO and ITO solutions for international clients.

- The lifestyle features of Altia have led to an employee group that is thrilled to be working in such high-quality, comfortable conditions. Their enthusiasm leads to high productivity and lower levels of attrition.

- By and large, clients that come to Altia stay. They rely on the 24-7 support, assistance with hiring, and customized services to meet their every need.

- It may not be easy to build during times of unrest, but the payoffs—from satisfied clients to productive workers who remain in Honduras—have made it well worth the effort.

- Creating systems that are free from government involvement can lead to sustainability. You'll avoid the risks of being dependent on infrastructure that may not be reliable. You'll also steer clear of corruption and the disruptions it can cause.

CHAPTER 5

Envision the Transformation

I will never forget the time I first laid eyes on the city of Campeche, in the state of Campeche, Mexico. It wasn't my first time in Mexico. Indeed at GK we had been looking at different options in the country where we could set up a facility. We had scoped out northern regions in proximity to the US. In those areas industrial hubs dominated the scene. Contamination hung heavy in the air. We had looked at other cities in the central part of the country. To the south, Cancun and its economic potential had been explored too.

Back then, now more than two decades ago, the North American Free Trade Agreement (NAFTA), signed by Mexico, the United States, and Canada, had recently come into effect. This treaty eliminated most taxes and tariffs on goods imported and exported by each participating country. Clearly Mexico held opportunities for manufacturing expansion. GK aspired to open textile plants in the country, with an eye for expanding into other segments such as agriculture and real estate.

The question was *Where in Mexico?*

The quest to find a pertinent location brought on different recommendations and several trips. While many of these leads had potential, none of them seemed quite right—that is, until Campeche rose to the surface of one conversation. After that I couldn't shake the place from my mind.

The appeal didn't stem from glossy brochures or detailed presentations about the region. Quite the opposite. Campeche, it seemed, was off the well-traveled tourist paths. It wasn't a center for industry. However, from what I heard, it had the assets to become a manufacturing center. There was a young and growing workforce there. Land was available, and the economic indicators pointed to opportunity.

First, of course, we had to find Campeche. When we did we realized just how basic an infrastructure it had! Moreover the people were not used to standard business hours. We would need to build roads, plants, and offices. We would also have to transform a sleepy community into a working one.

It would take a transformation. And that's exactly what I set about to do.

Once I was aware of these factors, a vision formed in my mind. I could clearly see advantages for GK. We could spur on the local economy as well. It would take a transformation. And that's exactly what I set about to do.

In the following sections, you'll learn about GK's founding in Campeche. We'll go through the history of the region to provide context. As you observe the transformation, consider how it compares to your own strategies. Finding a low-cost place with great tax incentives, coupled with a forecast for growth, could be your company's ticket to profitability.

Learning about Campeche

When one hears of Campeche, one might ask, as I did, "Where is that?"

Let's start with an explanation. Campeche is in southern Mexico, near the tourist-saturated area of Cancun. It is just a short flight from Honduras to the south. It's possible to drive from Honduras to Campeche in one day.

While it may frequently be overshadowed by other glossy destinations in the Yucatan Peninsula, the state of Campeche has its own *encanto* (enchantment) that lingers with visitors. Its capital, also called Campeche, has long been inhabited. Mayans first lived there. Evidence of their activities remains today. In addition to trading with nearby groups, the Mayans likely fished in the calm waters along the outskirts of the bay. Agriculture abounded to support the people.

In 1540 the Spanish arrived in Campeche and were attracted to its location. The region makes up the western end of a fertile plain, with hills and slopes that overlook the quiet coastline of the Bay of Campeche. At the time, the Mayan settlement, which once flourished, had already declined due to unknown reasons. Fewer residents lived there compared to the centuries in the past.

The Spanish built over the Mayan village known as Kimpeche. They set up the new city as a trade center. The port town thrived during the following years. It served as a key point along an important trade route. Settlers discovered logwood trees that produced a valuable red dye. This commodity further increased the level of trade and wealth in the area.[38]

The bustling commerce—especially that of the coveted red pigment—drew the attention of others. Pirates, in particular, were attracted to it. They attacked the port city repeatedly. In 1663 a group viciously slaughtered its residents. The Spanish responded, building extensive walls around the city to provide protection.[39] The structures created an enclosure resembling an irregular hexagon from a bird's-

---

38 History.com Editors, "Campeche," updated August 21, 2018, https://www.history.com/topics/mexico/campeche.

39 Britannica, "Campeche: Mexico," accessed September 15, 2022, https://www.britannica.com/place/Campeche-Mexico.

eye view. It took eighteen years to complete. The perimeter extended more than eight thousand feet, and the walls were over twenty-six feet high.[40]

Mexico as a country gained independence from Spain in 1821. The city of Campeche officially became the capital of the state in 1862. During the eighteenth and nineteenth centuries, wealth poured into the city, a result of the significant trade that continued to pass through the area. Fishing and agriculture had their place. However, these activities were not as prominent as the commerce segment.

THE CHANGING ECONOMY OF CAMPECHE

The Mayan presence waxed and waned, and the pirates came and went. In a similar vein, commerce has fluctuated since Campeche became a capital and state. As trade shifted to other ports, the people of Campeche returned to the way of their roots and ancestors. Fishermen ventured into the waters. They filled their boats with catches to feed their families. Farmers plowed their land, planted crops, and harvested food for their households.

In the 1970s change rippled through the coastal waters and land. During that decade oil fields were discovered in the Bay of Campeche. This spurred activity for both the region and the country. PEMEX, Mexico's state-owned oil company, built infrastructure in the region to support its drilling operations.[41] Initially the production fueled economic levels.

Unfortunately, in 1979, an explosion occurred at the Ixtoc I platform, a PEMEX-run exploratory oil well in the Bay of Campeche. A fire ensued, causing the rig supporting the drilling to collapse and sink. Oil gushed into the sea. It took nine months to stop the leak.

40   History.com Editors, "Campeche."

41   History.com Editors, "Campeche."

When it finally halted, more than three million barrels of oil had spilled into the ocean.

The disaster affected much more than the PEMEX operations. Sadly sea life dwindled. Long after the spill disappeared from headlines, marine figures remained low. "The amount of fish to catch was never the same as before the spill," Pablo Bonastre, a veteran fisherman who remembered the accident, told the BBC in 2010.[42] He went on to explain what it was like to go out fishing after the incident. His comrades and he would catch fish. They pulled in creatures that had red eyes bursting out of their bodies.

With fewer catches available, some fishermen left the work on water and moved inland. The balance shifted. The people of Campeche grew to value agriculture and self-sustainment. Black marks—traces from the devastating spill—are permanently painted on the rugged rocks of the Campeche coastline.

It's possible the region would have adopted other economic activities in the following years if opportunities had been available. However, there was little to no industry or business besides the oil production. Individuals who wanted a chance at a better life found themselves wishing for one—without anything tangible to grasp or use toward achieving that goal.

EMBEDDED IN THE PAST

Remnants of Campeche's rich history remained. In 1999 UNESCO designated the city center of Campeche as a world heritage site. This marked its significance and contributions to historical events during previous generations.[43]

---

42 Julian Miglierini, "Mexicans Still Haunted by 1979 IXTOC Spill," BBC.com (BBC News, June 14, 2010), https://www.bbc.com/news/10307105.

43 Britannica, "Campeche: Mexico."

In a nod to its past, the city features colonial buildings, fortifications from the seventeenth and eighteenth centuries, and access to nearby Mayan ruins. Less than an hour by car from the city lies Edzna, an archaeological site featuring a five-level temple. The formations of Uxmal, with its renowned Pyramid of the Magician, rest two hours away. The state has nearly one thousand registered archeological sites, including Calakmul, an abandoned Mayan city nestled deep in the jungle.[44] It is thought that Calakmul once housed fifty thousand inhabitants at its peak during the sixth and seventh centuries. About six thousand buildings and ceremonial structures remain in the now silent, but not forgotten, city.[45]

ENTERING A FISHING VILLAGE

It was this setting that my eyes rested on as I gazed out the window of the rolling vehicle, during GK's first trip to Campeche. At that time a dirt road led to the sleepy fishing village and wound past the signs of yesteryear, the landmarks of a long, complex history. I was entering a remarkably different world compared to the congestion and crowdedness of cities like San Pedro Sula, Honduras. In contrast this serene place basked in sunlight and the beauty of the nearby coastline. Hammocks dotted the scenery. Fields of crops spread out over the landscape.

There was no manufacturing in the region. Indeed I saw no sign of infrastructure to support machines and buildings. There were few souls in sight during my initial midday ride through town. I wondered, *Where are they?*

Turns out, the people were taking their siesta. They lounged through the warm hours of the day. With no set schedule, and the only

---

44   Michael Snyder, "In Campeche, Pyramids Are Everywhere. Crowds Are Not,"
      New York Times, February 2, 2018, https://www.nytimes.com/2018/02/02/travel/
      campeche-mexico-pyramids.html.

45   History.com Editors, "Campeche."

necessities consisting of providing food for the current day, workers essentially created their own pace. The town had lulled into a routine of rest at sunset. The villagers labored during the early portions of the day. Then they ate a meal and had their downtime. After the siesta they would change clothes (if they could afford the luxury). They would welcome in the cooler, breezy evenings. Certainly this was not a place accustomed to nine-to-five office routines or eight-hour stretches of factory work.

A Turnaround

Rather than walk away and turn to some of the competing areas I had seen in other parts of the country, such as the well-equipped northern industrial hubs or the sprawling metropolis of Mexico City, GK decided to stay and invest in Campeche. The challenges were great: there were no established commercial utility lines and no solid transportation routes. Essentially the city and surrounding area lacked the necessary infrastructure for manufacturing centers. The inhabitants lived a laid-back lifestyle that did not include packing a lunch and punching the clock.

Yet there were opportunities too. I saw a chance to have operations relatively close to GK headquarters in Honduras. The proximity to water made it accessible for shipments coming in and going out. Thanks to NAFTA, international companies were looking for partners to help them set up operations in Mexico. There was geographic room to begin and grow. Finally, and of utmost importance, there were people to help.

While fishing and agriculture may sound like—and certainly are—noble activities, the harsh reality is that in today's connected and advanced world, these basic activities, performed on an individual basis, leave little room for earning potential. The fishermen I found in Campeche didn't always have a home of their own. They couldn't afford it. If they did have one, it might consist of basic cement blocks, with blankets and tarps draped for doors. Children who wanted to study and learn often had to turn down those educational aspirations. Instead they worked to help support their family. Even if they weren't needed at home, occupations like agriculture didn't provide enough income to cover their school supplies and transportation. Their future … was not full of possibilities.

I looked around Campeche and met with the people there. I watched the children forage for scraps. I passed individuals on the street asking for food.

Without a doubt, this was the place to be. I envisioned the transformation waiting to take place. GK could provide jobs, wages, an income to support higher learning, a paycheck to provide more than a mere day's supply of food. Opportunities to help abounded … They were merely waiting for someone to act. We would.

OPENING DOORS

Fast-forward with me from my first visit to Campeche to a point in time when we had filled out all the necessary paperwork to start operations. We had overseen the construction of the infrastructure for our textile operations. We had worked with government officials to develop an economic and industrial plan. We would bring more jobs to the city and to the state of Campeche.

During that start-up phase, we looked for ways to collaborate and instigate change. We spoke with community leaders to learn of the needs of the people. We put a shovel into the ground, confident that our green practices would be implemented to improve—rather than destroy—the surrounding environment.

A strong, charismatic influencer was needed to drive the changes that would shape Campeche's people. The leader would give them a new lifestyle to think about. The person in power would also help families begin to create their future.

I wanted a team member who was familiar with GK's culture and practices. Alfredo Flores had been working at GK in Honduras for some time. Full of passion and energy, he had shown both dedication to service and motivation to succeed. During his time with the company, he had quickly risen in rank. He was the perfect fit for taking on the reigns of a new GK in Mexico.

When they heard of new jobs available, complete with competitive benefits and higher-than-average pay, they came from near and far.

Alfredo agreed to move, along with his family, from Honduras to Campeche. There he would help establish a GK presence. He would be closely involved in the effort to transform the fishing village and agricultural-minded society.

One effect of GK's efforts became clear almost immediately. Individuals wanted to work. When they heard of new jobs available, complete with competitive benefits and higher-than-average pay, they came from near and far. Hiring took place to staff a textile plant, with promises to build other facilities and provide more job opportunities.

Like projects in other developing areas, the new facilities did not turn into a quick fix for the region. Nor were the efforts obstacle-free. The first hurdle involved bypassing the afternoon nap and keeping steady hours. As Alfredo recalled, "At first, employees would show up and work the hours they were given. They would stay until their first paycheck. Then they would disappear for a few days, missing work."

When they received wages, they stayed away from the job and spent the cash. They might go out for an evening, purchase new clothing, or improve their living quarters. When the money ran out, they would return to work. For instance if they were paid on Friday and scheduled to work again the following week from Monday to Friday, they might not come on Monday or Tuesday. On Wednesday, with an empty pocket, they would return. Getting paid on a regular basis and being accountable to a schedule was a foreign concept.

Alfredo and others at GK explained to these individuals that the agreed-upon hours were meant to serve as a contract between the employee and the company. The workers would show up and carry out the tasks at hand. In exchange they would receive wages for their work. They could spend some of the funds and save other portions. Regardless they would need to return to work for their following shift. They couldn't wait until their next needed meal arose. This approach called for a shift to their lifestyle. It took considerable time and effort.

ATTRACTING NEW PARTNERS

GK established a plant and then a full industrial hub and other facilities in the region. As in Honduras, GK's team provided turnkey solutions for clients in need of space, equipment, and a labor force. Staff members took care of all legal matters and worked with local leaders to ensure seamless production and distribution. GK soon expanded into other areas of the state, including the town of Calkini, situated in the northern tip of Campeche.

During that time other companies expressed interest in operating there. One of these partners, Harper Industries, a US apparel manufacturer, turned to GK for assistance in establishing a presence in Mexico. The seventy-five-year-old firm was undergoing a transition at the time. For the first fifty years of its existence, the business operated in the US. When it became less competitive to produce there, the company became an importer. Then it decided to move its manufacturing to Mexico. While searching for a place to set up a facility, the firm's manager came across GK.

The manager saw how GK had transformed the region. The location was ready for more to come. Much of the hard work had been done already. It would be easier for partners like Harper Industries to establish a presence there.

In addition GK could help the company learn the ropes of the newly renovated area. "It's very difficult to be in a new place," explained Thomas Friedland, head of the company, which is based in California. "The easiest thing is to do something you've done before. The next easiest is to role model after someone in your family. It's harder the further away you go and the greater the differences in culture."

GK took care of all matters related to setting up the company in Campeche. Today Harper Industries produces apparel at three factories, employing more than two thousand workers. It supplies products such as sportswear, baseball caps, team sports uniforms, and medical garments to retailers in the US, Canada, Mexico, and other countries.

Creating New Livelihoods

Was it the right move to delve into Campeche? Was all the work needed for the transformation worth it? In hindsight the initial efforts paid off. The number of jobs in the area increased dramatically. Companies with facilities in the region noticed the change too.

When Tom took his wife, Sandy, and their grown children to tour the plant in Campeche, the trip began with apprehension. "The kids were quite worried about what they might see, anticipating poor working conditions and assuming that workers were being exploited," Sandy remembered. "Our young skeptics quickly saw that the factory was beautiful and the people working there appeared happy, healthy, and engaged in their tasks."

Alfredo showed Sandy and her children around the facilities. After, he reflected on the previous years and initial efforts at GK in Mexico. "When we opened the factory, applicants were lined up outside as far as I could see, hoping to be hired," he recollected. "Many of them were dressed in rags. Now look at them: they are well dressed, they have a steady income, and most of them now own houses. Not big ones, but concrete, sturdy homes. Some of our workers even have two because they married another employee." He then explained how the state of Campeche offers workers who can show a set number of months of pay stubs an almost interest-free mortgage to buy a house. In addition there are provisions for suspending the mortgage payments should a worker get sick or lose his or her job.

OVERCOMING SKEPTICISM WITH TRANSFORMATION

What is the best approach to take in a region burdened with a history of conquests, of rifts, and a sense of downfall? Surely eyebrows must have been raised when GK first entered the state. Longtime residents, whose ancestors had tread along the same paths and worked the underlying fields, were keenly aware that previous settlements had come and gone. The Mayans were born, rose to become a powerhouse, and then declined in numbers. While their DNA remains, the people of a different era are no more. The Spanish forced their entry in turn, and the pirates fought for control over key commodities. Tremors of oil spilled into the sea still wash their way to the shores of Campeche.

GK set out, as it has in other places, determined not to relive the history books that have been written. Instead the company sought to build and create a new, better place. In addition to increasing jobs and reducing poverty in the region, GK has focused on enhancing the ecosystem. One of its initiatives, Palma Real del Sureste, consists of an agricultural development to produce African palm oil. It carries out sustainable planting, cultivation, and processing methods. Along a similar vein, Campeche Oil Mills is dedicated to the responsible processing and producing of fresh palm fruit, crude palm oil, and crude palm kernel oil.

GK now has numerous projects in the region, including Campeche Industrial Hub with ready-to-use, customized solutions for clients with 24-7 support. It also created Ocean View Hotel, the first business hotel in the city of Campeche. Across from a lovely boardwalk, the property is a five-minute walk from the historical downtown. Next to the hotel is a fast-food establishment, which GK initiated—the first of its kind in the town. Lines can often be seen in front of the place, as customers wait to receive their order—which they can pay for, take home to their families, or enjoy in the pleasant atmosphere of the restaurant.

GK is behind Campeche Hills, an exclusive residential complex located in one of the most elevated areas of the city. It captures the essence of natural beauty and the elegance of urban life. It features scenes of the lovely coastal surroundings and lush vegetation, hallmarks of the region.

The story of GK's expansion didn't end with Campeche. Instead it extended operations to other countries in Central America and the Caribbean. It has a presence in El Salvador, Guatemala, Nicaragua, the Dominican Republic, and Pakistan. Its business units include textile, real estate, lifestyle, technology, and agriculture.

In every place we've gone, GK has looked for ways to create a transformation. I start with a vision of what could be—and then make it happen. I use what I see, such as trade incentives, local trends, and interest in industrial development. I then set about to maximize those qualities. In doing so the entire landscape changes for the better.

HOW TO DO BUSINESS IN DEVELOPING COUNTRIES

- Don't be quick to relocate. Take the time to explore various areas. You'll gain long-term benefits from the extra up-front research.

- Before creating an initial contract to build, make sure your vision is firmly in place. Run it past others to get their input. Modify it to adapt to the needs that arise during the start-up phase.

- Think carefully about location. If you want to be next to the US, for instance, you'll still find a multitude of options. Countries like Mexico are vast and have many possibilities.

- Don't underestimate a labor pool that is eager to earn a better wage. You can offer a salary that is slightly above average for the area. Workers pay attention, and compensation is a great contributor to employee satisfaction.

- If a local economy is open to your industry, show them what you can do. Focus on the improvements you can make for their area. Point out the jobs you can bring in through your company.

CHAPTER 6

Prioritize Education

Come with me on a journey that is a bit different than the tour we took during the first chapter. This trip consists of an inspection to a school in rural Honduras. Perhaps it can serve as a conversation starter, a beginning point for our exploration into the realm of education and developing countries. Through the tale it is my hope that you may come to see a glimpse of the challenges and opportunities that await us. It will also serve to demonstrate the basis for GK's strategy in dealing with this global, present, and ongoing issue.

The story begins at dawn, in the rolling hills of a less populated region of Honduras. An inspector sets out, ready for the day's work. This supervisor has been charged with the task of monitoring and observing government schools in the area. On the list for today is a small, two-room cabin nestled in the mountains. It is run by one teacher and has about fifteen students. The instructor must travel in from a larger city to reach this place. As such, the teacher has a small quarter set up in one room of the school. There is a bed, a small dresser, and a desk in the living space. The other room is used for teaching the smattering of students.

Through the government system, the teacher is supposed to receive a salary every two weeks. In return it is expected that the teacher will travel and stay during the week at this remote village. There are no paved roads in the area. Utilities are scarce. The population lives in poverty and has high illiteracy rates. The government-provided lodging is more accommodating than the other options in the area.

The concept has good intentions. The idea that the teacher can provide an education to a portion of citizens who otherwise may not have the opportunity to learn is admirable. Increasing literacy in the area could motivate young people to look for better jobs. They may be compelled to stay within the country and work rather than migrate.

This account, however, is not altruistic. It is more real to life. In this instance the inspector sets out on horseback. Once he arrives at the two-room school, complete with living quarters for the instructor, the air is still. It is a school day. No one is to be found within sight of the building.

The inspector enters the school, which is unlocked. Both rooms are completely empty. There is one noticeable feature that stands out in the space. The inspector runs a hand along a desk, then the doorknob, and moves to the other room. It is in the same condition. The living quarters, like the school room section, is covered in dust.

When were classes last held? the inspector wonders. Also, *Where is the teacher?*

You can fill in the rest of the story based on logical conclusions. It is likely the inspector went to the nearby village and made some inquiries. Perhaps a school-aged child, unaware of the issues at hand when government officials visit and teachers skimp on duty, shares that no classes have been held for two weeks. Maybe a mother approaches the inspector and pleas for help. She knows education is the only opportunity her children will have to improve their lives. She cannot afford to send them to another place for school. She is fully dependent on what the government can provide. When those provisions don't include instructors and regular learning sessions, the future for little ones begins to dim.

Herein lies a smattering of challenges that we find in developing countries. The problem isn't unique to Honduras. In areas stricken with poverty, the government might not pay wages to the educational staff. Workers may not be held accountable. Schools can lack resources like school supplies. Children often drop out to work and help at home.

For this reason GK Foundation takes a specific approach when starting any education-minded project. It focuses on constructing and remodeling classrooms at schools. This doesn't have to be carried out in a singular, massive overhaul. Instead classrooms can be changed one at a time. With each school year, a classroom can be repainted. Supplies can be brought in, ranging from new desks to books, coloring tools, counting blocks, and so on. When this happens, students and teachers alike tend to feel the difference. Suddenly they are in a bright, freshly painted room that seems vibrant. Indeed it is a place that exudes energy and positivity.

As you lay ground in a new country, don't overlook the power of education.

Along a similar line, GK Foundation makes general improvements in school infrastructure. It ensures that teachers in rural areas are paid competitive wages. It gives scholarships for private colleges and universities to outstanding students. It sponsors innovative and tech-related projects to further enhance educational quality.

As you lay ground in a new country, don't overlook the power of education. As history has shown, it holds the key to further development. When people receive an education, they can get a better job. Maybe they could fill positions that you will need someday in your company. GK is committed to prioritizing education, and I encourage you to do the same in your endeavors.

Let's spend some time looking at the difference access to high-quality education can make. We'll focus on areas where GK has been involved and seen an impact. These include Honduras, Pakistan, Mexico, and the United Arab Emirates (UAE). We'll look at each in turn.

Education in Honduras

One of the cornerstones to progress in the global economy is a skilled labor force. This consists of workers who can create, adopt, and adapt to innovation and technology. In Honduras there is a paradox between the investment in education and the results. Government expenditures on education are above average for the region. However, the youth literacy rate and human capital index are below the regional norms. On average, citizens of Honduras have five years of schooling.[46]

At a global scale, Honduras ranks poorly for educational access and levels. Its Human Capital Index was listed in ninety-third place out of 130 economies, according to the World Economic Forum.[47] Its challenges include illiteracy in rural populations, where two out of ten people cannot read. The country suffers from low access to secondary schools and scarce enrollment in postsecondary educational institutions. Sixty-three percent of the labor force only has a primary education. Among workers, 81 percent are concentrated in the agriculture and manufacturing sectors.

---

46   USAID, "Honduras: Country Profile vs Region," accessed September 13, 2022, https://idea.usaid.gov/cd/honduras?comparisonGroup=region.

47   Manuel Orozco and Marcela Valdivia, "Educational Challenges in Honduras and Consequences for Human Capital and Development," The Dialogue, February 2017, https://www.thedialogue.org/wp-content/uploads/2017/03/Educational-Challenges-in-Honduras-FINAL.pdf.

Nearly half of the ten million people living in Honduras reside in remote, mountainous villages sprinkled throughout the country. For a child who wants to study beyond the sixth grade, the trip to school will often include a long walk down the mountainside to the nearest road. There the student will hitch a ride with others to the closest highway. Then they will get on a public bus. The transportation system will take them to the nearest city with a school. When class ends, the child will return the same way. In all, the transportation time to get to and from school can take three to five hours.[48]

Students from remote areas who want to study high school often must live away from home, simply because there are no options in their neighborhoods. They might stay with friends or family members in one of the larger cities that has a high school, such as Danli, Yuscuran, Zamorano, San Pedro Sula, or Tegucigalpa. Or they could go to a weekend school and bring home assignments to do throughout the week. Their weekdays would consist of working with their parents at home or in the fields. At night they would do homework.

The government provides education for the public through sixth grade. Still there are costs tied to uniforms and school supplies. Families are frequently unable to afford these basics. Only 51 percent of children who begin elementary school complete it. If they do finish, it often takes nine years to finish six grades. This is due to the need to occasionally leave school and assist the family. Among those who get through the lower levels, only 30 percent begin attending high school.[49]

---

48 Honduras Good Works, "Problems with Education in Honduras," accessed September 13, 2022, https://hondurasgoodworks.org/?page_id=141.

49 Bless the Children, "A Study of Education in Honduras," accessed September 14, 2022, https://www.blessthechildreninc.org/index.cfm?page=EducationFactsHonduras.

Even before the pandemic, the crisis related to education was evident in the country. Out of the nearly 2.4 million children who were of school age, 14 percent were not receiving any type of formal education. El Código de la Niñez, which serves as the official code for the protection of children, states that every minor under the age of eighteen has the right to receive an education. Still the public educational system faces many challenges. The quality of academics is lacking, more so in rural areas. Teachers go on strike from being overworked and undercompensated. Many public institutions fall short on technical training. Children are typically not provided with school supplies or textbooks.[50]

The pandemic further escalated ongoing issues. Shutdowns prevented children from studying. Many did not have access to tablets or computers to study online. Those that did have equipment often lacked an internet connection. Power outages, instituted by government policies, caused disruption. For most public-school children, the academic year was effectively lost. Among those who dropped out, a fair share will never return to school.

Instead they will become child workers for their families. Or they will turn into "street children," digging through garbage bins in search of food. They will beg at stoplights. In worst-case scenarios, they will join gangs and face the risk of violence, prostitution, and drug abuse. *Pandillas* (gangs) teach members that the way to earn a living is through crime. After all, for many, it is the only route they see available. Street children are considered among the poorest and most marginalized groups in Honduras.

---

50   Rita Michelle Rivera, "Public Education in Honduras: How the COVID-19 Pandemic Exacerbated an On-Going Educational Crisis," *Trauma Psychology News*, November 13, 2020, https://traumapsychnews.com/2020/11/public-education-in-honduras-how-the-covid-19-pandemic-exacerbated-an-on-going-educational-crisis/.

OPENING DOORS THROUGH ENGLISH

In Honduras, English is not taught in the public school system. Those that attend the government programs do not gain exposure to vocabulary, songs, literature, and spoken communication. English is the language of the world. It is typically a required skill to connect and interact with international companies.

Would it be possible to create bilingual schools that would be free and open to the public? It is a question we pondered at GK. Rather than dreaming about a place that could be accessible or handing out funds to children to attend these environments, we developed a project that would work hand in hand with local governments and infrastructure. It wouldn't disrupt neighborhoods or place children in settings where they were not comfortable (such as a child from an impoverished sector attending a high-end, private school, where they might be subject to teasing and feel out of their comfort zone).

We became the first company to turn basic educational centers into top-notch, high-performing bilingual schools.

GK Foundation decided to take on the challenge. We became the first company to turn basic educational centers into top-notch, high-performing bilingual schools. An initial step toward achieving this goal involved creating an alliance with the ministry of education in Honduras. Through this partnership each party has a certain set of responsibilities.

The government is accountable for

- Ensuring and promoting collaboration to uplevel the quality of education for all students.

- Providing facilities where students can learn.

- Staffing the project with school directors and Spanish-speaking teachers.

- Providing authorized diplomas for the foreign language educational system.

- Supporting future efforts through similar methodology.

For its part GK Foundation is responsible for

- Selecting a top-rated bilingual teaching method.

- Hiring qualified English teachers.

- Building and remodeling classrooms where English will be taught.

- Providing all the teaching materials needed.

- Monitoring class quality.

- Organizing and providing logistics for graduations.

When one enters a renovated school, the atmosphere is lively. Putting our initial story against one of these educational institutions is somewhat like comparing night and day. In the rural, abandoned school situations, there is little hope for a better life. The families know it. Inside a free bilingual school, the children are learning English every day. They're going to a place that is fully staffed with accountable teachers. Their parents can learn too. Everyone involved in the project is aware that, one day, the students who graduate from these schools will be able to fill out a job application and check the box that states, "English Skills." These positions pay more than factory jobs and offer a ladder. Young people can build a career, a life, and a better way of living.

The project aims to provide world-class bilingual education to children of low-income families. It ensures that students who participate in the English program receive a language certificate that is approved by the Honduran ministry of education at elementary, middle, and high school levels. These steps help turn the dream of providing better opportunities and a professional future into a reality.

In Honduras there are four public schools that are 100 percent bilingual as a result of GK Foundation's efforts. These have been remodeled, staffed with bilingual teachers, filled with books by US publishers, stocked with teaching materials, and even given a computer lab. Children who walk into these places nearly dance upon entering. Their parents look on in wonder, marveling at the opened doors that await their children. In a world fraught with danger, crime, and low reading levels, these institutions are a true ray of sunshine.

The project is ongoing. Every year new students are enrolled in kindergarten and preschool levels at these schools. As children advance, grades are opened to the bilingual system. GK Foundation ensures that once children have started, they can continue to study all elementary levels and continue into secondary and high school—even on to university levels.

In addition GK Foundation has taken on projects to support public schools that are Spanish focused. Each of the companies under the GK umbrella selects a nearby school. The foundation then assists with teacher wages to ensure consistency. The foundation helps improve the infrastructure. It also carries out wellness campaigns and special celebrations.

Why not offer English in all schools, if that is what is needed? you may be asking. It is a good question. At GK we realized that our commitment to the community must meet citizens at all levels. It is a large task to take on a school and implement an English language program, complete with staff and a continuous curriculum. Since education is a priority, each project needs to be designed and carried out at a top-level standard. This involves resources of time and funding.

As such, it's simply not possible to take all the public schools in Honduras and immediately renovate their structures, staffing, materials, and programs. Efforts can be made little by little. Every bit counts. Each step forward is a move in a positive direction.

Perhaps the most significant benefit of prioritizing Spanish schools in the surrounding areas of our companies lies in the community aspect. We treat our workers like family, and we want what is best for them. That includes the options they have for their children's education. By helping the schools close to them, their school-aged family members and neighbors have a chance to attend a high-quality, well-run, operating school. There are more than five Spanish public schools that have been receiving support from GK Foundation.

BEYOND EDUCATION

It takes family support to send a child to school. As we've seen, children are often at risk of being put in the labor force. Even in cases when parents want to help their son or daughter learn, the process can put a financial strain on the household. With that in mind, GK carries out efforts to build up families. It helps members in need find a job.

These endeavors include workshops with trained staff. Topics include current and relevant topics such as environment care and how to handle bullying. Activities are regularly held to maintain Honduran customs and traditions. Informative meetings are scheduled for parents to discuss domestic violence and social risks. There are regular celebrations and festivities at the schools, which serve as gathering events. Qualified professionals are brought in to provide training for English and Spanish teachers. There is a "Reconnect" program to provide psychological help as well.

EduKarims

For adults who never had the chance to finish elementary levels of schooling, not all doors have closed. GK Foundation offers adult education in communities surrounding its facilities. It also provides training projects, development opportunities, and career plans for employees.

An assistance program known as EduKarims benefits employees first and foremost. It recognizes their value by supporting their basic education and helping them achieve academic growth. For workers who have not completed higher levels of secondary and high school, this program gives them access to classes so they can finish. If they want to continue studying at the university level, it supports their efforts.

Silver Matamoros, a cleaning supervisor at GK, did exactly this. "Since I was a child, I had the dream of one day being a professional engineer," he stated. "But for me conditions did not come together, and I had lost all hope of achieving it." He found a job at GK and quickly felt like he had found a new family. Through EduKarims he finished middle school. "The graduation was awesome!" he recalled. Silver didn't stop there; he went on to study high school and pursue his dream of becoming an engineer.

Others have noticed GK's work and its collaboration with government institutions to create synergy. "GK and its foundation are characterized by demonstrating commitment and social responsibility with the development of people," said Isaac Ferrera, director of Institutional Development for Latin America and the Caribbean Panamerican Zamorano University. "GK and its foundation have contributed to support Zamorano students in need of a scholarship to achieve their goal of becoming professionals and positive leaders of change for society."

Access to education is one of the most critical obstacles for human development in Honduras. In the country approximately one million young people do not have opportunities to work or to study. This is significant and timely, as the average age of the population of Honduras is twenty-four years old.[51] According to official figures, of the 1.5 million students who go to school, only 33 percent will finish sixth grade.[52]

Given these statistics, GK Foundation shines as a beacon of hope for all the children enrolled in the schools it supports. By attending, these students are increasing their chances of finding employment and earning a steady salary later. For their families the school represents an opportunity for the next generation to rise, both on an individual level and for society at large.

Education in Pakistan

Approximately 22.8 million children between the ages of five and sixteen do not attend school in Pakistan. The figure represents 44 percent of the total population in the age group. With statistics like these, the country has the world's second-highest number of out-of-school children.[53]

A multitude of factors merge to create obstacles for children attending school in the country. These include supply-related issues.

---

51   Worldometer, "Honduras Median Age," accessed October 8, 2022, https://www. worldometers.info/world-population/honduras-population/.

52   USAID from the American People, "Performance Evaluation: Honduras Workforce Development," February 2019, https://pdf.usaid.gov/pdf_docs/PA00TVMT.pdf.

53   UNICEF, "Pakistan: Education," accessed September 14, 2022, https://www.unicef. org/pakistan/education.

School facilities are not available in some parts of the country. There are economic factors too. Paying for education is not a possibility for the very poor. Access is an ongoing challenge, and more boys than girls attend school.[54]

THE CITIZENS FOUNDATION

"We thank you for believing in young people and the transformative value of education."

—**Isaac Ferrera,** *principal of institutional development for Latin America and the Caribbean Panamerican Zamorano University*

Through the Citizens Foundation (TCF) in Karachi, GK helps to run more than 1,650 schools throughout Pakistan. TCF works to create positive change by removing barriers of class and privilege. It embeds schools in the center of urban slums and rural communities. It uses female teachers with a fifty-fifty student gender ratio. The schools are well equipped with airy and well-lit classrooms, an administrative section, playground, library, and computer and science labs. The buildings stand out as landmarks in their communities. They create a stimulating environment in which children are motivated to learn.[55]

Asad is one of the students who has benefited from the Citizens Foundation (TCF). Asad comes from a small, mud-brick home on a dusty street of Karachi. There is often no power in his residence. Every day, insects buzz about. A leaky roof is a way of life. His father had to drop out of school at a young age to work and support his family. Now a fruit seller, his income isn't sufficient to send his five children

---

54   UNICEF, "Pakistan: Education."

55   The Citizens Foundation, "The Citizens Foundation: Our Schools," accessed September 14, 2022, https://www.tcf.org.pk/our-schools/.

through school. Through TCF, Asad and his siblings did not have to step away from education to work and support the family.[56]

Asad finished high school and went on to study for a university-level degree. "In our community, boys are expected to take up full-time jobs at a young age, but Baba (father) encouraged me to focus on my education," he shared. "When I was leaving for university, he handed me some money for my living expenses which he had been saving to get our roof fixed. When I hesitated, he told me, 'The repairing of our home can wait but this opportunity might not come again.'"[57]

Asad went on to graduate from college specializing in technology, ready to begin a career in software. His two younger brothers and two younger sisters continue to study through TCF's help. All of them have big dreams of their own.[58]

"Thank you GK for opening a world of opportunities for me!"

—**Silver Matamoros,** *cleaning supervisor and participant in EduKarims*

ADDITIONAL EFFORTS IN PAKISTAN

GK Foundation is a sponsor for the Namal Knowledge City, an exciting initiative for quality education. It prioritizes rural communities. Based on leading examples such as Oxford and Cambridge, this project is directed toward creating a knowledge economy in the heart of Pakistan. It is the first of its kind in the country to unite knowledge workers from around the world. It features sustainable development, including academic blocks, libraries, technology parks,

---

56   The Citizens Foundation, "Fruit-Seller's Son, TCF Alumnus Graduates from GIKI," August 10, 2022, https://www.tcf.org.pk/2022/08/fruit-sellers-son-tcf-alumnus-graduates-from-giki/.

57   The Citizens Foundation, "Fruit-Seller's Son."

58   The Citizens Foundation, "Fruit-Seller's Son."

business centers, dairy farms, primary and secondary schools, sports facilities, a hospital, shopping centers, hotels, and housing for staff, faculty, and students.[59]

Namal is situated in an atmosphere that evokes the aura of green it wishes to maintain. The vision for the city includes protecting the natural, social, and physical environment, especially that of Namal Valley. This geographic point lies amid mountains and has a unique topography. Namal Lake has a surface area of approximately five square kilometers. It is the most prominent feature of the region. It is surrounded by smaller bodies of water.

The economy in the area is largely agrarian. Namal Valley is a sanctuary for migrant birds and animals that thrive in its comfortable ecosystem. The nearby lands serve as grazing pasture for animals, creating scenery that is serene, inviting, and calming.[60]

Beyond these efforts, in Pakistan the GK Foundation

- Equips women with skills and microenterprise support. More than 2,400 have received instruction through these initiatives. They learn a vocation, which they can then teach to others and use to serve in their communities.

- Provides scholarships for underprivileged local students who want to study at the Habib University and pursue higher educational goals.

- Supports the Halima Amdani Campus through a variety of educational initiatives to improve student performance, encourage diversity, and develop children.

59 Namal Knowledge City, "Namal Knowledge City: An Inspiration, a Dream," accessed September 14, 2022, https://namal.edu.pk/namal-knowledge-city.

60 Namal Knowledge City, "Green Namal," accessed September 14, 2022, https://namal.edu.pk/green-namal.

The efforts in Pakistan face challenges, including those from the natural environment itself. In 2022 floods raged through parts of the country. Rising water significantly impacted the provinces of Balochistan, Khyber Pakhtunkhwa, and Sindh. Heavy rains over the course of several months caused landslides and flash flooding. Thousands of people lost their homes.[61] After the rains one-third of the country was submerged in water.[62]

These occurrences further motivate GK to continue its efforts. When children are educated, they can grow up and get a better job. They might receive a higher paycheck that allows them to live in a sturdy home. They can better protect themselves and their families from the impact of a natural disaster.

Education in Mexico

In Campeche, Mexico, GK Foundation supports public schools. It provides them with teaching equipment and materials. It also helps improve the educational infrastructure.

Like other areas of Mexico, Campeche faces several barriers to quality education. These include the pervasive problem of low income: about 18 percent of the country lives in extreme poverty. School dropout rates, absences, and grade repetition are ongoing issues for Mexican students in poor regions. The country has one of the lowest rates of enrollment for young people between the ages of fifteen and

---

61   Shah Meer Baloch, "Pakistan Floods Kill 580 and Bring Misery to Millions," *The Guardian*, August 17, 2022, https://www.theguardian.com/global-development/2022/aug/17/pakistan-floods-kill-580-and-bring-misery-to-millions.

62   Anmol Irfan, "Pakistan's Flood Disaster Shows the Perils of Climate Shortsightedness," Foreign Policy, September 14, 2022, https://foreignpolicy.com/2022/09/14/pakistan-floods-disaster-relief-climate-change/.

nineteen. This sector of the population is often driven to find jobs rather than finish school.[63]

Mexico is home to indigenous communities, which tend to be poorer than nonindigenous groups. These people struggle with cultural gaps, discrimination, and being taught skills that are not relevant to their way of life. Mexico's spending on education as a country is lower than the OECD average. Girls over the age of twelve are more likely than boys to drop out of school.[64]

Education in UAE

In 1995 His Highness (HH) Shaikh Rashid Al Maktoum Pakistan School was established in Dubai. The consulate general of Pakistan in Dubai founded the school to meet the needs of the Pakistani expat community. GK served as a sponsor of the project. The school's slogan, "Every Child Is a Winner," reflects the focus on high achievement and performance. The school's vision is to raise diligent, lifelong learners who are responsible citizens and respectful individuals. The institution emphasizes an environment where children feel loved and encouraged.[65]

The Positive Impact of Education

Astrid Marbella Castellón Contreras, a student at Armenta GK Foundation bilingual school in San Pedro Sula, Honduras, shared her thoughts when she was in eighth grade. "First of all, I want to thank

---

63   ICF, "4 Barriers to Quality Education in the Mexico School System," June 20, 2022, https://icfdn.org/barriers-quality-education-mexico/.

64   ICF, "4 Barriers to Quality Education."

65   His Highness Shaikh Rashid Al Maktoum Pakistan School Dubai, "Vision and Mission," accessed September 14, 2022, https://www.sramps.sch.ae/vision-and-mission/.

God," she began. "I'm grateful to GK Foundation because they have given me the opportunity to study English since I was in kindergarten. I have been enjoying nice experiences since I was six years old with my peers and my teachers."

Being able to speak and write in English was not an accomplishment Astrid expected from early on. Rather, through her training at the school, she was able to learn the language. As her ability grew, so did her motivation to continue in her studies. "When I was six years old, I was talking with my peers," she recalled. "I told them that even though learning a second language would be a challenge, we can achieve this goal."

Eager to excel, Astrid led her students through each passing school year. "I always have been a very dedicated student. When I first started to learn English, it was both exciting and difficult."

This one skill opened Astrid's eyes to a new future, one flush with the chance to grow, explore, and keep on improving. "For my family and me, being part of this project represents a lot because it has changed our lives in many ways. I want to keep on learning English and maybe study abroad."

Like GK, the UN prioritizes education. The SDG 4 lists education for upward socioeconomic mobility.[66] I invite you, as you set plans, to join this initiative. Helping even one child to learn more can positively alter the trajectory of their career.

---

66   United Nations, "4: Quality Education," accessed September 14, 2022, https://www.un.org/sustainabledevelopment/education/.

HOW TO DO BUSINESS IN DEVELOPING COUNTRIES

- To prioritize education start by understanding the local infrastructure. Observe what is available to everyday people. Talk to authorities and directors to understand their challenges.

- Seek out ways to collaborate when carrying out educational projects. Nonprofits, governments, and schools may be eager to participate in a well-laid-out approach.

- Start small and use trial and error to learn best practices. Once you've found a strategy that works, seek out ways to expand efforts.

CHAPTER 7

Show Empathy in Healthcare

I n Pakistan a child dies every minute.[67] Poverty and health inequality permeate the country. More than 16 percent of the population is under five years old. Many infants and toddlers lack access to clean water and preventative care. Pakistan is in the bottom 5 percent of countries in the world in terms of spending on health.[68]

According to UNICEF the under-five mortality rate in the country is seventy-four deaths for every one thousand live births. Conditions in Pakistan are reflective of those in low-income countries. Many of the deaths are preventable if treatment is given on time. The issue, then, is two-fold: a lack of awareness and a need for resources.

Consider the stark difference that occurs in a developed nation. A mother takes her four-month-old daughter to a scheduled appointment. While there the pediatrician examines the infant, checks vital signs, and gives the all clear, an indication that the child is in good health. The mother and patient have visited before, and all their records are on digital file at the medical facility. A nurse distributes

---

67   ChildLife Foundation, "ChildLife Foundation: Homepage," accessed September 9, 2022, https://childlifefoundation.org/.

68   Fowad Murtaza, Mustafa Tajammal, and Rabia Awan, "Child Health Inequalities and Its Dimensions in Pakistan," *Journal of Family and Community Medicine* 22 (September-December 2015), no. 3: 169-174, https://doi.org/ 10.4103/2230-8229.163036.

the immunizations that the child needs. Records are updated accordingly. On the way out, the mother pauses at the front desk and talks to the receptionist for a few minutes. She is told her insurance will cover everything from the visit. The receptionist looks at the records, which indicate when the next regular visit is due. An appointment in two months is made.

Prior to the next visit, the mother will receive a text message from the medical center to remind her of the upcoming appointment. She will be told of any preparations to make. She may also read about the immunizations her infant needs, how to care for her during these months, and how to monitor her nutrition and sleep. If anything seems off before the next visit, the mother will reach out to the clinic. She might talk through an issue with the nurse, schedule a visit to have her daughter checked, or go to the pharmacy to purchase baby supplies.

Perhaps during this in-between time, the daughter runs a fever. The mother watches her closely and treats her with over-the-counter medicines like infant paracetamol (often seen as the brand Tylenol) and children's ibuprofen. The high temperature continues for several days, so the mother places a call to the doctor's office. After speaking to the medical staff, a nurse invites the mother to bring her child in to be checked. After examination, the doctor believes the child has an infection. A prescription for antibiotics is written and sent over to the pharmacy near the child's address. The mother heads home. The pharmacy where the prescription is filled delivers the medicine right to her doorstep.

On the day of the next appointment, the mother will show up at the doctor's office, ready to go over the next steps of her daughter's medical journey. The doctor will ask follow-up questions regarding the antibiotic and its treatment. The medical staff will want to know if the symptoms have eased and if all the medication was taken as directed. The mother will assure them that she followed the instructions as indicated regarding the medicine. She will note that her child did not have any allergic reactions and that the symptoms have dissipated. The checkup will continue, following a similar pattern as the previous one. Heart rate, weight, and height will be checked. Immunizations will be distributed. Another appointment will be made on the way out the door. The cycle proceeds.

This story may seem mundane in the developed world. The case is even somewhat stereotyped. By and large, societies in these nations expect the majority of children to be vaccinated and treated for diseases. There are specialized centers if health conditions change and a child needs extra care, such as a surgery, long-term treatment, or developmental help. Services are available for neurological disorders or chronic conditions. The government often has programs to provide social aid to homes, where counselors and therapists work one on one with infants and children.

Now let's return to Pakistan and the situation there. Infectious diseases, which can often be cured with antibiotics, claim the lives of children on a regular basis. The households of these children may not be near a medical facility. Families in poverty often cannot afford to travel to a clinic. If they live close to medical care, they might not be able to pay for the needed medication. At a clinic they may be treated by staff members who have not had the opportunity to fully study common diseases. Health workers might not understand how to diagnose and treat frequently seen conditions.

In a developing area like Pakistan, an infant might not have the immunizations needed to protect them from disease. Mothers frequently lack knowledge about preventative care measures. An infant who develops a condition that needs antibiotics, such as a fever with flu symptoms, could go untreated. In Pakistan, ninety-two thousand children die of pneumonia every year. The illness accounts for 16 percent of total childhood deaths in the country.[69]

Coming into a country to help is not as simple as showing up and distributing medical supplies for several weeks or months. While this may sound appealing and attract volunteers who want to make a difference, the long line of challenges they face can result in suboptimal, or even dire, consequences. The obstacles to providing sustainable medical assistance in low-income countries include staff-related issues, relief work ineffectiveness, and a negative impact to the local population.

> *Creating access for everyone is the foundation. You can then build in high-quality care and patient experiences to uplevel health in poor areas.*

For these reasons it's important to approach healthcare the right way. When working in developing countries, I have found that empathy resolves myriad issues. Creating access for everyone is the foundation. You can then build in high-quality care and patient experiences to uplevel health in poor areas.

Barriers to Health Access

Aid workers coming from developed countries could face living conditions that are very different than what they consider normal. They may find undrinkable water, a lack of food, substandard lodging, unsafe transportation, extreme weather, a plethora of insects, rabies-infested

---

69   ChildLife Foundation, "The ChildLife Story," accessed September 11, 2022, https://childlifefoundation.org/our-story/.

animals, civic instability, and political unrest. These workers could have trouble accessing online resources and making phone calls, due to poor telecom infrastructure. They could be asked to work long hours. They may treat a seemingly never-ending flow of patients. They might operate in an inadequate facility that doesn't have consistent electricity, proper machines, equipment, or medications.[70]

If there are medical resources in the area, volunteers may be unfamiliar with their brand name and use. There could be different standards of care that don't align with their educational background. They may have difficulties communicating with patients due to cultural or language barriers.

Moreover the medical project itself isn't always suitable for the country. For instance short trips or workshops might have no follow-up. As such, patients don't receive continued treatment or monitoring. Activities that function outside of the local healthcare system often create a disjointed impression and are unsustainable. If there is no educational component to a project, local staff may be left with medications they don't know how to distribute.

The local population can be harmed by medical projects. When healthcare workers arrive, if they are not self-sufficient, their presence could drain regional food sources. This is especially true in disaster areas, where shortages tend to be prominent. Their visit could also absorb local water resources and shelter to the point that community members are left without. If a volunteer falls ill, their treatment could be a potential burden to the local hospital system. Health projects that provide free treatment and medicine could cause other local clinics that charge for care to suffer. In this

---

70   Christopher Van Tilburg, "Controversies in Medical Aid to Developing Countries: Balancing Help and Harm," *International Health* 7, no. 3 (May 2015): 147-148, https://doi.org/10.1093/inthealth/ihv028.

way the economy could take a downturn due to the presence of well-intentioned volunteer efforts.[71]

Aid workers can carry out activities that discourage patients to continue with care. For instance if a healthcare volunteer arrives in a rural area with immunizations, the local population may be unaware of their use. If there is no available infrastructure to keep the medicines at a controlled temperature, the immunizations could be ineffective. In rural Amazon areas, some tribes have adapted practices and a belief system that views vaccinations as dangerous. A worker who brings immunizations and their own method of refrigeration could still have little effect. Parents may refuse to have their children immunized. Even in cases in which vaccines are distributed, if they fall outside of local schedules or lack follow-up, children will be left with an incomplete protection system against disease.

Creating Access

Due to these risks, it is increasingly important for volunteer and aid groups to be in tune with how the local economy operates. They must know the available infrastructure, the resources at hand, and community norms regarding medical practices. When a system is developed to cooperate with local medical facilities, the potential for a positive impact is higher. On a similar note, programs that work in conjunction with local resources tend to be more effective. Adding an educational aspect encourages long-term functionality.

GK Foundation has put time and resources into ensuring that barriers are broken down. One of its core projects consists of being a founding sponsor to a nonprofit in Pakistan called ChildLife Foundation. We'll look at how it works and its impact next.

---

71   Van Tilburg, "Controversies in Medical Aid."

REDUCING INFANT MORTALITY RATES

ChildLife Foundation uses cutting-edge systems and healthcare innovations that are adapted for low-income areas to carry out medical work in Pakistan. It looks for communities that have been untouched by healthcare services, overlooked by the public sector, and unable to access private care. It provides emergency room care, along with primary care and preventative practices.

The ChildLife Foundation has created more than twelve state-of-the-art model emergency rooms in Pakistan by partnering with local resources. Its operations are in the following locations: Civil Hospital, the National Institute of Child Health, the Sindh Government Hospital Korangi-5, Lyari General Hospital, and Abbasi Shaheed Hospital in the city of Karachi; People's Medical College Hospital in Nawabshah; Chandka Medical College Hospital in Larkana; Ghulam Muhammad Mahar Medical College Hospital in Sukkur; Sandeman Provincial Hospital in Quetta; Liaquat University of Medical and Health Sciences in Hyderabad; Mayo Hospital in Lahore; and Pakistan Institute of Medical Sciences in Islamabad.[72]

The ChildLife Foundation also operates thirty-plus primary care clinics in the slum areas of Karachi. This is carried out in partnership with SINA Trust, a nonprofit organization that provides primary healthcare to underprivileged areas in Karachi.[73] In addition, it runs a preventative healthcare program that has reached more than one hundred ninety thousand families. All of these are comparable to the top levels of private medical care available in the country. In many cases, the technology it uses is more advanced. However, measures

---

72   ChildLife Foundation, "The ChildLife Story," accessed September 12, 2022, https://childlifefoundation.org/our-story/.

73   SINA, "About SINA Health Education & Welfare Trust," accessed September 12, 2022, https://www.facebook.com/SINAPK/.

are taken to ensure it is possible to use the technology and maintain it long term in the facilities.[74]

As a trustee member of the ChildLife Foundation, GK has overseen the expansion of its facilities and presence in Pakistan. Its mission is to save the future of Pakistan. These patients have been exposed to malaria, pneumonia, diarrhea, and birth problems related to malnutrition.

A HISTORY OF INNOVATION

ChildLife started its work in 2010. It began by adopting pediatric ERs of tertiary government hospitals. These are the hospitals where the poorest children are brought for treatment. In each place it adopts, the nonprofit's team members carry out three steps. First they bring in needed equipment and auxiliary support. Then they add resources including staff and pharmacy. Finally they develop processes including a paperless system. This creates an ER that is digitalized and automated. The system can be used to measure protocols.

The organization follows the international standards of three Cs for care. These include a competent staff, compliance according to international protocol, and compassionate treatment. These three pillars are used to deliver quality care to the sickest and poorest children in Pakistan.

The impact of ChildLife can be measured in several ways. Starting in 2018 the organization has provided sufficient care in Karachi so that every child is within thirty minutes of an ER. This provides peace of mind to poor parents in Karachi. The survival rate of children under its care has risen from 20 percent to more than 80 percent. Patient satisfaction rates at ChildLife ERs have been recorded at 73

74   ChildLife Foundation, "The ChildLife Story."

percent, which is higher than international standards. The under-five mortality is the lowest in the province of Sindh in Pakistan. This location is where ChildLife has been working for the last ten years.[75]

Throughout its years of existence, ChildLife has received recognitions. It was granted the Best Corporate Report Gold Award by the South Asian Federation of Accountants. The foundation operates under the objective to create access to quality emergency care that is available 24-7 and completely free to all children.

The Importance for Pakistan

While these figures indicate signs of progress, another approach to viewing the difference that ChildLife has made starts by understanding what life is like in Pakistan. We'll begin with Karachi. We'll then consider the countryside. Finally we will observe how ChildLife, which began in Karachi, is reaching out to cover as many children as possible throughout the country.

A VISIT TO KARACHI

Karachi is the largest city in Pakistan. It is the capital of the Sindh province in the southern portion of the country. The metropolitan area holds more than sixteen million people.[76] Karachi is home to a major seaport on the shores of the Arabian Sea. Its air travel development and foreign business attraction have made the city an important part of the country's economy. In addition Karachi is a massive commercial and financial center. It has been compared to New York City.

---

75   ChildLife Foundation, "CEO Message," accessed September 12, 2022, https://child-lifefoundation.org/ceo-message/.

76   Macrotrends, "Karachi, Pakistan Metro Area Population 1950-2022," accessed September 12, 2022, https://www.macrotrends.net/cities/22044/karachi/population.

It has a magnificent nighttime skyline with an array of brilliant colors splashed against a dark evening background.[77]

Visitors to the city will find modern supermarkets, beautiful architecture, luxurious shopping malls, high-end eateries, city tours, and museums showcasing historical artifacts.[78] Karachi is home to the expansive greenery of Bin Qasim Park, which covers 130 acres and is the biggest family park in South Asia. The getaway features a turtle pond and stone canopies, along with hundreds of thousands of unique rose saplings.[79]

Beneath these headlines there is another side of Karachi. This one is much bleaker. It consists of dark twists and turns, of a quicksand-style of life … meaning that once a person is in it, getting out is a strenuous, often hopeless task. Roads in the city are congested. The public transportation system is expensive for the majority of the city's residents. With few low-cost housing options, the poor drift toward the slums. Once there, they stay.

LIFE FOR THE UNDERPRIVILEGED

There are more than six hundred slums in the Karachi region. Approximately 65 percent of the city's population, or nearly two out of every three people, live in poverty-stricken places. In these sections garbage piles up. The dirt streets are lined with basic mud-and-brick structures. In some cases blankets and tarps separate living spaces from the eyes of passersby.

---

77   Emma Fellows, "10 Facts About Poverty in Karachi," The Borgen Project, May 10, 2018, https://borgenproject.org/10-facts-about-poverty-in-karachi/.

78   Trip Advisor, "Things to Do in Karachi," accessed September 12, 2022, https://www.tripadvisor.com/Attractions-g295414-Activities-Karachi_Sindh_Province.html.

79   GPS MyCity, "Bagh-e-Ibne Qasim Park, Karachi," accessed September 12, 2022, https://www.gpsmycity.com/attractions/bagh-e-ibne-qasim-park-32409.html.

Among the devastated plots, Orangi Town, the world's largest slum, stands out. It is home to more than 2.4 million people.[80] Comparing a child living in this section to one dwelling in a modern high-rise is heart wrenching. Think of a child who is in constant search for food and water, with little access to education and healthcare. Then imagine a scene in which a lad wakes up every morning in a bed, then saunters down the hall of an apartment to the dining area, where house staff members have just finished putting out the family's breakfast.

In the slums, water is often short. When it is available, it is usually not safe to drink. Those who ingest it are prone to waterborne diseases, including pneumonic-type illnesses, skin diseases, and diarrhea. Children are especially at risk. Farmers on the outskirts of the metro area, in a desperate search for irrigation sources, sometimes use water mixed with sewage lines. The produce that is then harvested is polluted and unsafe for consumption. When people eat the vegetation, the consequences can include severe illness.[81]

The city's conflicted sector was brought to international attention in 2010. At the time, severe flooding left 20 percent of Pakistan underwater and affected twenty million people. Many were left homeless and without access to clean water. A lack of sanitation, food, and healthcare made the outlook dim. Stagnant pools of water led to an intense plague of dengue, the worst the country had ever seen.

In August of that year, Dr. Sanjay Gupta, chief medical correspondent for CNN, went to report on the disaster. Soon a new flood began. This time it consisted of images portraying a Karachi in

80   Jai Shah, "5 Facts about Orangi Town: The World's Largest Slum," The Borgen Project, November 4, 2019, https://borgenproject.org/orangi-town-the-worlds-largest-slum/.

81   Emma Fellows, "10 Facts about Poverty in Karachi," The Borgen Project, May 20, 2018, https://borgenproject.org/10-facts-about-poverty-in-karachi/.

ruins to the public audience. Viewers watched patients lying on the floors of medical centers. There were no beds for them. Worse, due to a medicine shortage, care was a mere thought—not an action that could be delivered. The scenes were disturbing.[82]

A group of Pakistani businessmen saw the report. Upon viewing it, they were moved to solve the crisis. They formed a collaboration with the government. Soon they began renovating the Civic Hospital's Emergency Room for Pediatrics in Karachi, a 1,900-bed tertiary care public hospital. The institution is also one of the largest teaching hospitals in Pakistan. It provides both undergraduate and postgraduate training.

This collaboration led to the formation of ChildLife. Its founders shared a dream to save every child's life through innovative solutions. The first endeavor led to a twenty-two-bed facility. The center has world-class features and a well-equipped pharmacy, along with a triage room.

FACING THE FUTURE WITH TECHNOLOGY

While it has influenced positive change in Karachi, ChildLife recognizes there is more to be done. Leveraging the advances of technology, it is working to increase its impact. A recent project, the ChildLife Telemedicine Satellite Center, reaches even more lives.

The driving force for this initiative lies in the distribution of Pakistan's people. Since so much of Pakistan's population lives far away from urban centers, there is a struggle to access healthcare. Through the telemedicine system, a doctor sits at a central site and is connected to secondary hospitals through screens. There are high-definition cameras installed at the remote sites. The physician on call reviews

---

82   ChildLife Foundation, "What We Do," accessed September 12, 2022, https://childlife-foundation.org/what-we-do/emergency-care/.

cases. The doctor then remotely guides nurses at the rural location to help them distribute the right treatment for the patient.

For developing countries, telemedicine satellite centers greatly increase access for patients living in rural areas. They enable health workers in these regions to receive a second opinion about critical conditions. They allow patients to be monitored and to receive follow-up appointments. Telemedicine satellite centers are also cost effective, as staff members do not need to travel out to these hard-to-reach areas.

ChildLife uses a hub-and-spoke network to cover as much area as possible. This consists of a center location, which then reaches out digitally to points that fall within its circumference. The system has increased the level of available care in remote regions.

Nearly half of the patients who visit ChildLife ERs have problems that could have been avoided. The foundation

> *For developing countries, telemedicine satellite centers greatly increase access for patients living in rural areas.*

believes that prevention is better than the cure. For this reason it developed the preventative health program. Through it staff members teach patients about safety measures. Visitors are registered via phone for the program when they arrive at the ER. They are then sent messages about the importance of washing hands, vaccination, breastfeeding, and other child health matters. The information is prerecorded and sent via robocall, which can be cost efficient and effective in countries with low literacy rates like Pakistan.[83]

The start of this Pakistani nonprofit stems from tragedy. The severe flooding motivated a group of leaders to reverse the difficult

---

83 ChildLife Foundation, "Preventive Care," accessed September 12, 2022, https://childlifefoundation.org/what-we-do/preventive-care/.

situation. Over the years their efforts have gained traction. For many the gift of medicine and treatment brings healing and life. The opportunities to reach more, supported by advanced and sustainable technology, are exciting. And they represent the exact type of project GK Foundation seeks: one that emulates empathy and creates access.

HOW TO DO BUSINESS IN DEVELOPING COUNTRIES

- When bringing in volunteers to help with healthcare, do initial research to see what challenges they could face. If possible, incorporate their efforts into long-term programs that are already in place.

- Start new projects with a sense of empathy. Look for what the main healthcare issues are in the area. Keep well-being in mind as you develop plans.

- Don't get overwhelmed in places with intense needs. Look for a way to break in, such as treating children with antibiotics. Over time you may be able to add more services, like surgery and treatment plans.

- Remember that equipping patients and their families with knowledge can help them prevent future conditions. It is also a way to show a personal touch. They'll see you care enough to help them with their ongoing needs.

CHAPTER 8

Work toward Health Equity

In a developing nation, when a medical need arises, a patient often has two choices. They can opt to go to the government clinic and receive treatment there for free. Or they might choose to pay for private services, which can be costly for many.

While in theory the free government care may sound like a simple solution, the reality is that these systems often include long waits and limited supplies. The medicine needed to treat a condition may not be available. A patient might have to undergo surgery to get better. This could entail a wait of months, a year, or longer.

Let that last phrase sink in for a moment. Say you have a ten-year-old son who isn't feeling well. You take him in to the government medical clinic very early on a weekday morning. You sit in a patient waiting area the entire day. This arrangement is commonplace in developing nations. Your case is classified as not urgent (i.e., not life threatening). It is deemed that he can wait. You and your son stay all day without visiting a doctor. When the clinic closes, you go and spend the night at the house of a nearby relative.

The following day you return and see a general practitioner. After several rounds of testing and more waiting, it is determined that your son will need to see an oncologist. The first appointment available is six months from now. The secretary assures you that sometimes the wait is much longer. Six months is considered a good option.

Sadly at this point you are aware that your son likely has cancer and will need treatment. You also know that he is going to have to wait six more months to start a program to fight the disease. During that time you understand that the cancer could spread. Even after the treatment begins, if surgery is needed, the wait could stretch out for more months and even a year.

That's a typical scenario for the first option, the public version. The other choice involves going to a private clinic. These facilities are not run by the government. They do, however, charge fees.

The benefits of these private clinics are that they are often attentive. They offer quick service and high levels of care. Among the drawbacks, the most significant one in developing countries comes down to cost. Prices are often set to cover doctor salaries, worker wages, and expenses related to the facility. The worker who earns an average wage cannot afford a private clinic.

It's up to you and me to find a bridge that connects the very poor with high-quality care. I've worked on strategies during the last decades to do exactly that. At GK Foundation we've sought ways to close the gap between the "haves" and "have nots" in healthcare. We uphold nutrition and share the UN's goal to reach zero hunger.

Let's explore the different areas where GK Foundation is at work to bring health equity. We'll start in Honduras. We'll delve into projects underway in Mexico and other places. As you review them, think of how you could set up initiatives to instill health equity in the countries where you have a presence.

Care on Demand

Through GK Foundation, healthcare and dental assistance are provided to employees and their families. Every year the group holds health fairs, along with medical and dental brigades, in the neighboring communities of all GK companies. Through these, every year thousands of people receive the treatment they need.

Thanks to alliances with international organizations, including the nonprofit Hands Helping Honduras, GK Foundation bridges the gap between healthcare needs and treatment availability. Professional volunteers identify infants, children, and adults who require urgent medical attention. Doctors and surgeons from other countries come to help provide care to these patients. Some of the specialties covered include cardiology, orthopedics, and general surgeries.

For many these brigades and health fairs are the ticket to getting a better life. This is especially true when the other choice, due to limited resources, is to wait. In such a case, a person's health could further deteriorate before treatment begins.

To those who are not connected with international care, GK Foundation offers other options. Every year it donates medical equipment, beds, transport stretchers, X-ray panels, thermometers, stethoscopes, and fabrics for making healthcare apparel. It supplies outpatient and intrahospital medications. It helps provide treatments for chemotherapy and other critical conditions.

QUALITY CLINICAL CARE FOR ALL

Known as *Clinica Medica Amar y Compartir* (Love and Care Medical Clinic), this GK-run facility lies in the outpatient area of a public hospital in San Pedro Sula, Honduras. When patients first enter the hospital, they are evaluated to determine their level of care. The public portion of the hospital offers medical emergency services. Patients who need immediate assistance are admitted. Those who come and do not have an urgent condition can be referred to the Love and Care Medical Clinic.

Referred patients that enter this charitable wing of the hospital receive attentive care. For many it is the first time they have been treated humanely in a public hospital environment. Some appreciate the caring attitude so much that they return, even after their treatment has ended. In these instances they show up just to continue the relationship. The staff operates in a first-class clinic, aiming to deliver friendly and personalized services to all.

> *For many it is the first time they have been treated humanely in a public hospital environment.*

To date, the clinic has treated more than one hundred thousand patients. Each one has received medical attention at no charge. They have been given all the medicine needed to treat their condition. Some of the services provided include dental and social assistance, gynecology, pediatric care, and general medicine.

Elevating Low-Income Care in Mexico

In Campeche, Mexico, there are shelters and orphanages, along with rehabilitation centers, that don't have the resources needed to purchase food for those in their care. GK Foundation has stepped in, distributing balanced and nutritious staples to these groups. It also gives meals to some of the schools in the area that are underbudgeted. More than five hundred people are fed every day.

GK also supports Una Caricia Humana Shelter in Campeche, Mexico. This organization assists low-income cancer patients both in the state and surrounding areas who are looking for help in Clinicas Medicas Especializadas (CME). At these centers patients receive free oncology treatment, regardless of their background.

DISTRIBUTING AID DURING THE PANDEMIC

In early 2020, when tremors of a disease rippled through countries and wrapped their tentacles around the globe, Honduras and Mexico reacted akin to other developing countries. Uncertainty abounded. For countries with limited resources, the consequences of Covid-19 came swiftly and were more severe than in other developed areas. When the virus hit in full force, the walls of the hospitals nearly burst. Every bed held a patient. Lines waited outside.

By August 2020 a survey in Latin America and the Caribbean found that 71 percent of low-income respondents had a household member who had lost a job. Among small businesses, over 60 percent reported that a person in their family closed their business. Food security and overall health declined. This created a snowballing challenge for populations living in poverty.[84]

At GK we witnessed the effects of the pandemic firsthand. When households hovering around the poverty line lost a source of income, they didn't have money to buy food. If there was an illness, there were no funds available to purchase medicine.

Imagine for a moment that it is 2020. You live in Mexico and have a job in a factory that is not run by GK. With the income you bring home, you support an elderly parent, a spouse, two children of your own, and two nephews you have adopted because

---

84   Nicolas L. Bottan, Bridget Hoffmann, and Diego A. Vera-Cossio, "The Unequal Impact of the Coronavirus Pandemic: Evidence from Seventeen Developing Countries," IDB, August 2020, https://publications.iadb.org/en/the-unequal-impact-of-the-coronavirus-pandemic-evidence-from-seventeen-developing-countries.

their parents are absent. Your spouse works as a cleaner in homes three days a week. You are the main breadwinner. You need $300 a month to pay for all the bills, provide food and clothing, and cover transportation costs.

You and your household live in a four-room cement-block home. Two of these serve as bedrooms. A third room is a family gathering place. The fourth is a small kitchen. There is a shared bathroom outside.

The home is in a community that has an open courtyard in the middle. Homes surround it, and there are several common places, including wash lines where the day's laundry can be hung to dry. Several dogs spend their days hanging out in the courtyard. During especially warm months, the children sleep outside in the open area. Most of the residents are relatives. The complex has been in the family for several generations.

When the pandemic hits, your spouse loses the cleaning work. Then your factory job evaporates. The government shuts down the plant because it produces nonessential items. The factory notifies you that it won't be paying wages to workers during the nonproductive time.

Now survey the scene once more. Look around at the children in the courtyard and the elderly parent sitting off to the side in the shade watching them. How will they be provided for? What sort of protection will they have from the pandemic? Where will the next meal come from?

These are the types of questions and scenarios that many in Honduras and Mexico, along with other developing countries, faced as wave after wave of Covid-19 pulsed through societies. With no income, no health protection, and no end in sight, the situation grew worse with each passing day. Many wondered how they would survive both the disease and the future, given their few opportunities.

Extending Aid to the Vulnerable

In addition to helping workers and their families, GK looked to communities. How could one's heart not be touched when looking out upon the hills and rows of low-income housing? How could one not feel compelled to lend a hand when so many were suffering?

Thanks to its manufacturing plants and foundation, GK had the means to help those in need. During the pandemic it donated biosafety equipment and medications to hospitals, humanitarian organizations, and individuals in the communities surrounding its operations. It gave more than fifteen million face masks and food bags to neighborhoods in Honduras, Mexico, Pakistan, and the US.

At GK efforts were refocused to the crisis response. We wanted to play a part in helping to reduce risks. We also wanted to support essential businesses. GK began producing pandemic-related goods, including isolation gowns. These are a type of personal protective equipment used in healthcare settings or in environments where disease prevention is key. Isolation gowns are especially helpful for vulnerable patients with weakened immune systems in hospitals. They were applicable in factories and ports for employees whose jobs involved direct contact with materials arriving from different parts of the world.

These gowns, at the time they were made, were an instrumental factor in helping global supply chains to continue. They came in two forms: washable fabric made of resistant cotton, or disposable versions formed of SMS plastic. By producing these, GK participated in worldwide action to mitigate risks associated with the pandemic.

Times of crises call for collective action. Companies that focus on progress, collaboration, and alliances can make a difference. At GK we brought in the necessary equipment to protect workers during their daily activities. We had doctors and medical professionals on staff, available to test employees and monitor their health conditions. We maintained salaries and wages. We kept workers and transitioned production to orders that aligned with pandemic-related needs.

If you were in the imagined scenario, with a household dependent on your wages from a factory job, at GK the story would have had a different ending. Rather than wondering where the next meal would come from, you would have had continued pay. Your job responsibilities and hours may have changed; yet you would have had the assurance you were participating in efforts to help fight the crisis at hand.

Natural Disaster Help in Honduras

In November 2020, as much of the country of Honduras was house-bound due to the pandemic, another disaster struck. On the fifth of that month, Tropical Storm Eta hit northern Honduras. A little more than two weeks later, another hurricane—this one named Iota—rolled through. The heavy winds and rain brought destruction to the communities surrounding San Pedro Sula, including Copan, Choluteca, and Comayagua. The storm impacted the departments of Puerto Cortes, Yoro, Atlantida, Santa Barbara, Olancho, and Colon. Some of the workers in the Green Valley Manufacturing Hub in Santa Barbara and Altia Smart City in San Pedro Sula, along with employees of other GK textile and spinning plants in the region, suffered losses from the hurricanes.

The Honduras government reported that approximately 4.7 million people were affected by these hurricanes. Of those, over 368,901 were isolated, and more than one hundred people died from the floods produced by the storms. Thousands of homes filled with water reaching up to two meters. In these cases all household items were lost. The majority of homes located along the Chamelecon River were completely destroyed. More than sixty bridges were wiped out, and over seventy were damaged. A total of 927 roads were affected too. The infrastructure damage caused communities that were difficult to access to be completely isolated for several weeks.[85]

The timing seemed especially painful, as the pandemic had already brought severe social and economic consequences to the region. The hurricanes were preceded by droughts in agricultural areas, leading to food insecurity. All these factors had increased violence and poverty levels in the country.

In short it was a moment of severe suffering for many who were already going through a hard time. Families looked for temporary places to stay, surveyed the damage and loss, and waited for the transportation routes to reopen. They needed the roads to access services and their jobs once more.

Not willing to stand on the sidelines, GK Foundation pitched in. It started by reaching out to employees that were impacted by the devastation to get back on their feet. It assisted them with rebuilding their homes. It helped the neighbors of employees go on with their lives too. It set up shelters for those who were waiting for new homes and supported hurricane victims with food and medicine. GK donated forty-six acres of land for thousands of families to use as a new starting point. It created houses for the stranded to call home. Hurricane victims started their lives again, with dignity.

NATURAL DISASTERS IN DEVELOPING COUNTRIES

According to the UN, many developing nations remain unprotected against disaster. They may not have built-in alert systems to warn

---

85 IFRC, "Honduras: Hurricane Eta and Iota—Emergency Appeal," January 21, 2021, https://reliefweb.int/report/honduras/honduras-hurricane-eta-and-iota-emergency-appeal-n-mdr43007-operation-update-no-2.

citizens of upcoming events such as hurricanes. This alone can have a severe negative effect. A message sent out a mere twenty-four hours in advance can reduce the damage by 30 percent. After the disaster hits, weak health systems and infrastructure can leave more vulnerable. In areas plagued with poverty, unplanned rapid urbanization, and biodiversity loss, the risks further increase. Disasters that strike these areas can do even more damage, ultimately demoting progress.[86]

The statistics are saddening and pose an important question to societies, to businesses, and to individuals. What can be done to help these areas? When stepping into a street in one of these regions, it may seem impossible to create change. You might come across crowded streets that appear full of chaos and lacking in order. You could see shacks on small properties, where a laundry line holds the day's wash. Shirts and pants hang to dry. In some cases this is the only change of clothes a person may have besides what they are currently wearing. Chickens might scramble under the clothes, pecking at the brown earth in search of scraps that have fallen from the outdoor table. The family living inside might not have any money saved for a rainy day. They are more likely to be living day to day, unsure at times of how the next piece of bread—let alone full meal—will come to them.

Rather than leaving us in a state of depression, the reality of natural disasters in developing countries sheds light on a larger issue at hand—one of improving the quality of living. As we've seen, job creation in these areas is often a stepping stone toward better conditions. Workers are more likely to remain in the country, and the household isn't separated as a result. This avoids issues related to broken homes, which often suffer financially and are more susceptible to violence and abuse. As employees receive wages, they spend

---

86   United Nations, "When Disaster Strikes, Developing Countries Still Too Vulnerable," UN News, October 13, 2021, https://news.un.org/en/story/2021/10/1102912.

funds in their communities, bolstering the nearby businesses and helping other citizens. As income levels spread and grow, a sort of rebirth starts to occur. You might see a shanty home. Next to it a cement block structure appears. Little by little the worker and their household are building a new home. The laundry outside disappears when a washer and dryer are purchased. The chickens are placed in a pen and fed well. When the stronger home is finished, the property is better prepared to face a natural disaster. You can imagine that the storm striking a cement-block home, rather than a metal and cardboard shack,

> *Better wages lead to improved conditions, which create stronger families and well-made houses.*

will do less damage. The spiral continues upward. Better wages lead to improved conditions, which create stronger families and well-made houses. The cycle can play out again, this time upleveling the quality of life even more.

Feeding the Hungry

After the hurricanes Eta and Iota, as poverty increased, GK reached out with a mission to serve the elderly, disabled, women, and children on the streets. It created *Alimentando Esperanza* (Nourishing Hope), a program that aims to help Hondurans who cannot afford a meal. Every week GK employees hand out a free lunch at noon to those in need. More than one hundred thousand dishes of food have been delivered since 2021.

GK Foundation also supports OBAT Helpers. This is a nonprofit organization committed to providing food, aid, education, and economic help to those in need in Bangladesh. Aid is given to the displaced and stranded in refugee camps.

In Karachi, Pakistan, where many live in low-income areas, GK supports the distribution of 1,500 cooked meals every day. It also helps provide ten thousand pieces of baked bread. These are handed out daily to those in need.

Helping in Other Areas of Pakistan

GK Foundation contributes to Indus Hospital & Health Network, a nonprofit that is located in the densely populated sector of Karachi called Korangi. It has a three-hundred-bed hospital that provides free care to everyone. The center has a paperless system. It has become a beacon of hope for the most fragile members of society.[87]

At the Korangi campus, GK Foundation provides support for four dialysis units. These perform an average of twelve dialyses every day and three hundred per month. For those who need treatment, the services create the opportunity to live another day.

In addition GK is one of the founders and a trustee member of the Memon Medical Institute, a nonprofit, 100 percent donor-funded hospital that exists to serve the underprivileged at no cost. Since 2010 it has treated more than sixty thousand patients every year. All its medical records are computerized. It covers an area of 320,000 square feet, is centrally air conditioned, and has its own power generation facility.

Among its achievements are the following:

- Fifty free medical camps in Karachi

---

87   Indus Hospital & Health Network, "About Us," accessed September 12, 2022, https://indushospital.org.pk/about/.

- Two-hundred-plus free knee replacements in adults

- Eighteen free cochlear implant surgeries to restore healing in kids

- One hundred free outpatient services every day

The Memon Medical Institute has participated in polio campaigns and in the national tuberculosis control program. It offers hearing screenings for infants. The facility also has postgraduate training programs to encourage the further education of medical staff in Pakistan.

GK contributes to the Patel Hospital in Karachi, a care facility that caters to those in need. It has a patient welfare program to provide high-quality healthcare to everyone, regardless of their economic status, race, creed, color, or religion. The services offered include cardiology, gynecology, burn care and plastic surgery, and kidney and bladder treatments.

Care for All in UAE and US

GK participated in the creation of the Pakistan Medical Centre, a project of Pakistan Association Dubai. Located in Dubai, it opened its doors in October 2020. The facility provides free treatment to patients of all nationalities throughout the UAE. It holds cardiology clinics, gynecology clinics, and pediatrics clinics. None of these has a charge.

In Miami Gardens, Florida, GK is a sponsor of many of the programs and activities of the United Heritage Institute (UHI) Clinic, which is a member of the National Association of Free and Charitable Clinics (NAFC). UHI provides a wide range of services to two million medically disadvantaged people every year. It caters to those who cannot afford medical insurance. Without insurance these patients face potentially high charges for going to other medical facilities, where outpatient services, prescriptions, and minor surgeries can cost thousands of dollars. In some cases, without places like UHI, patients would need to go to an emergency room for nonemergency care. Doing so creates high costs both for them and for the healthcare system.[88]

When individuals attend UHI, they receive assistance in primary medical care, chronic disease care and management, dental care, behavioral and mental healthcare, optometry, women's health, smoking programs, immunizations, pharmacy and medication access, health navigation, and other specialty care. The clinic treats between forty and fifty uninsured or underinsured patients every day.[89]

Beyond these services UHI has programs to develop future healthcare professionals and leaders. Students who are in a medical training program can sign up to help at UHI. In doing so they have the chance to see the needs of the community in an up-close, personal way. UHI also works with organizations to provide data about minorities and the underserved population in need of healthcare in Southern Florida.

When Mahmoud Sir sought help for his two sons in Southern Florida, he couldn't afford to take them to a clinic that charged for care. At UHI he found the assistance he needed for both of his sons' general health and vision care. "Their staff is friendly, accommodating, and inviting," he said. "They don't make you feel inferior. Their doctors and physicians in training are attentive, gentle, and patient-centric."[90]

Helping with healthcare access begins one patient at a time. To be effective, efforts account for local needs, barriers to access, and

---

88   UHI Clinic, "About Us," accessed September 12, 2022, https://uhiclinic.org/about-us/.

89   UHI Clinic, "About Us."

90   UHI Clinic, "About Us."

available resources. In times of disaster, every moment is critical. Having systems in place can allow organizations to reach out when it matters. As a result more lives could be saved.

In every place, from developing nations to first-world countries, there are health needs. At GK we've worked on finding them. We've developed programs to close the gap between those that can easily receive care and those that cannot. I hope these projects serve to inspire more to participate in the global movement. In your own way, you can help pave the road to health equity.

HOW TO DO BUSINESS IN DEVELOPING COUNTRIES

- Visit public healthcare facilities in the developing country where you are working. If possible go through as a patient. Try to see the experience through their eyes.

- In safe settings walk through poverty-stricken neighborhoods with health needs. Pay attention to what you see and hear. Ask residents what their challenges are.

- In areas that have higher standards of living, don't assume everyone has access to healthcare. Hand out surveys to see what struggles families face.

- Develop programs with a goal in mind. Do you hope you reduce health inequity rates in the area? If so, what is a practical outcome that could be reached? Once you have an objective, track and measure results so you can monitor the impact.

CHAPTER 9

Lean into Tech Advances

Lenin Palencia dreamed of a career in business. He wanted to run his own company and maximize the potential of technology. Raised by a single mother in a humble home in San Pedro Sula, Lenin was one of four children. They all needed to be fed and clothed. Resources didn't abound. In fact the opposite was true. Lenin grew up in a poverty-stricken household and community.

His story may have ended where it began—in poverty—had Lenin accepted the status quo. Rather than put his dreams aside, he got to work. He knew he would have to study and learn how to function in business and be a leader. He went with his mother to the local market. She sold goods there every day to bring in cash. He helped her peddle merchandise. In doing so he accumulated enough funds to cover the family's daily expenses—and still have some left.[91]

Through these activities, Lenin gathered the resources he needed for an education. He knew he was lucky; many of those in poverty can't earn enough to pay for school. Even if they do bring in an

---

91   Saúl Vásquez Vargas, "Exitosos e Influyentes Empresarios ha Formado el Intae Durante 40 Años," *La Prensa*, February 22, 2019, https://www.laprensa.hn/sanpedro/empresarios-intae-exitosos-san-pedro-sula-honduras-educacion-KBLP1261281.

income, they may have to use the money to support their family. If they get sick or injured, they could be out of work indefinitely.

In Lenin's case his mother encouraged him to use the resources toward his career. Getting an education took time and effort. In 1986 Lenin enrolled in the *Instituto Tecnológico de Administración de Empresas* (Technology Institute for Business Administration) in San Pedro Sula. He even brought merchandise to the campus and sold it there. He used the funds to buy books and cover school-related expenses.[92]

His dedication paid off. After graduating, he got a job at a major bank in Honduras. Lenin stayed with the financial institution for the next two decades. During his time there, his mind never strayed from his early goals of becoming his own boss.

He started looking for opportunities to pursue other business ventures. In 2003 he made an agreement with a friend who was involved in the auto industry. Lenin imported two used vehicles from the United States to Honduras. One was a 2001 white Geo Prizm; the other was a 2000 red Geo Metro. He brought the autos through the customs stations in Mexico and Guatemala and then transported them to San Pedro Sula. The cars sold quickly. The process opened Lenin's eyes to the value of knowing how to navigate border regulations, auto mechanics, insurance, and everything else involved with importing and financing autos.[93]

As a result Lenin thought about branching out on his own. Opening a new company, however, brought significant risks. Given his background he was familiar with a lifestyle in which one didn't know how the next meal would arrive. He didn't want to go back to those days. Still he couldn't shake the desire to have his own business.

---

92   Vargas, "Exitosos e Influyentes."

93   Grupo Amcresa, "Acerca de Nosotros," accessed October 13, 2022, https://www. amcresa.com/about-us.html.

During this time Lenin approached me and asked if we could talk. We had crossed paths during his early banking days. By then GK had a substantial presence in the country and was growing. Lenin, for his part, was known in the community. His story was one of success. After starting in poverty, he had worked himself to the position of vice president of a bank. His career and paycheck were set for life. He could look ahead to a comfortable retirement and better future for his family.

I agreed to meet with Lenin. He assured me he wanted a personal discussion—not a business-oriented one. While our previous encounters had been associated with finances and manufacturing topics, I told him I would talk to him friend to friend.

In our conversation he explained that he was grateful for his achievements. Yet he wanted to pursue a business opportunity that might involve leaving the bank. He was torn: How could he give up the comfortable salary for which he had worked so hard? How could he set aside his dream of being his own boss? At the bank he would never have the independence he sought.

I suggested going with his passion, but I put in one caveat: rather than use his lump sum toward the start-up, I encouraged him to set it aside.

I listened to Lenin's wrestling and his concerns over the future. I very much understood the frame of mind that comes with dreams, a vision, and objectives for the days ahead. I also empathized with his concerns over resources. He was looking at investing much—or all—of his savings into the new business. That would put him in a tough financial position. He would be at risk of losing it all.

Equipped with years of business experience, I shared the best advice I could with Lenin that day. I told him that I thought his goals were admirable and attainable. I suggested going with his passion and pursuing the auto-related financial venture. I put in one small, but vital, caveat. If Lenin stepped away from the bank, he would receive a stipend as part of his going-away package. Rather than use this lump sum toward the start-up, I encouraged him to set it aside. "Put it away," I said. "If something goes wrong with the new business, you'll still have more than enough to live comfortably for the rest of your years."

Lenin listened to me. The route wasn't easy. It involved more years of scrapping together finances for the new business. When he could have dipped into his savings and drawn from his own stash of resources, Lenin chose to follow my advice. With time his business boomed. He went on to become known in Honduras as a successful entrepreneur and influential businessman. Best of all for him, every day he could wake up as his own boss. He was living the life he dreamed of as a child.

I share Lenin's story here for several reasons. Certainly I am happy for him and the life he has achieved. His company, Grupo Amcresa, offers lines of credit and financing for vehicles. It also connects consumers to homes and helps them purchase residences to fulfill their own dreams. It is an important part of the Honduras economy and has created jobs for many workers.

Still there is a larger lesson to be learned from Lenin's tale. His trajectory shows us the benefits that technology and opportunity can bring to those who want a better life. Through his own videos, Lenin now encourages consumers to have a strong grip on their income and expenses. "Finances in order leads to happiness at home," he shares. He speaks the same advice at conferences, in

Facebook messages, and to anyone who sits in his office or spends time with him.[94]

Historically technology has held the key to enable individuals and communities to move up in life. It has provided a sense of hope for the future. It has enabled the middle class to rise and presented promises of prosperity for the next generation.

Taking advantage of these breakthroughs and putting them to good use can help bring more families out of poverty. At GK we've actively sought ways to increase the size of the middle-class population. I'm convinced these workers provide the engine that fuels a growing economy.

Let's look at the middle class and its historical context. We'll also cover tech needs and solutions. I'll share an example of how GK is working to tie these together. By providing tech skills, we can develop a growing middle class. In your area of expertise, you may find opportunities to carry out similar projects.

A Look at the Middle Class

When we consider three groups—low income, middle class, and wealthy—one stands out in terms of consumption. Currently the middle class is the largest spending group in the world. It makes up about half, or 45 percent, of the population. While there are different definitions for this segment, a common one identifies the middle class as anyone who earns between ten dollars and one hundred dollars a day.[95]

---

94 Tip Financiero, "Los Mejores Consejos con Nuestro Experto Lenin Palencia," accessed October 13, 2022, https://www.facebook.com/watch/?v=215650085781370.

95 Omri Wallace, "The World's Growing Middle Class," Elements, February 3, 2022, https://elements.visualcapitalist.com/the-worlds-growing-middle-class-2020-2030/.

In society, families that fall within the middle-class range tend to own a home where they live. They may have taken out a mortgage to fund the residence, which is likely their largest asset. Middle-class households typically can pay for their food, utilities, and transportation and have money to spare. They may use these extra funds to dine at restaurants or take occasional vacations. Parents in this category are often concerned for their children's welfare. They usually focus on education and skill development. Bettering the lives of the next generation and providing them with opportunities is important to them. Middle-class families are often tuned in to saving and have a long-term plan.

This differs from other segments of society, including the very poor. Those that make less than ten dollars a day do not have enough discretionary income to think about extra splurges. Vacation brochures will not adorn their coffee tables (if they can even afford the furniture). Instead there could be a stack of bills or eviction notices in the dwellings of the poor. Or there may be no paper at all, as is the case in shantytowns and makeshift homes built in urban slums. Household members may not be able to read or write. They might not have access to services like electricity and running water. The poor focus on providing food, clothing, and transportation for their households. In times of stress and need, these essentials are prioritized.

A child may be taken by bus to a hospital if they are seriously ill. Using these funds to pay for bus fare could mean that the family doesn't have anything left over for food that day. Due to the trip, purchasing a need such as a pair of shoes for a child might be put on hold indefinitely. The little one will then remain barefoot until footwear can be provided through earnings or other means, such as a donation. The poor account for just 6 percent of the total amount spent globally each year.[96]

On the other extreme, wealthy families do not have to contemplate how to bring in their next meal. This class is flush with funds and has discretionary income available for vacation homes, yachts, and the like. There is a spectrum to the segment, as not all households will be able to afford extended world travel—while others will. However, by and large the category is considered able to readily access the basics and beyond. A new pair of shoes can be bought without a second thought. Tuition for high-quality schools is paid, often in full and on time. Wealth discussions frequently center on passing an inheritance or legacy to future generations and maintaining the family's resources into the future.

The elite lead the world in terms of consumption.[97] Individuals with a net worth of more than $1 million make up approximately 1.1 percent of the world's population. They hold nearly half, or 45.8 percent, of global wealth.

In between these two classes—the poor and the wealthy—lie the middle-income earners. This class has risen in certain countries during the last decades. It plays an important role in the economy of a society. It provides the pulse needed to drive growth and generate more jobs.

A HISTORY OF THE MIDDLE CLASS

While inflation has caused wages to climb over the centuries, the concept of the middle class has remained similar since its origin. The segment first arose amid the Victorian era in England. As the Industrial Revolution ignited the nation and then the world, workers and positions were added at an alarming rate. Banks acquired clerks to

---

96   Wallace, "World's Growing Middle Class."

97   Wallace, "World's Growing Middle Class."

facilitate the machinery purchases that factory owners made for their manufacturing needs. These individuals earned the equivalent of what in recent times would be ten dollars a day.[98]

Similarly the goods that middle-class households purchase have remained the same. During the Industrial Revolution, the growing middle-income earners used their wages for lodging, food, clothes, and transportation. They carefully allocated additional funds, choosing between entertainment and other goods and services. Those that had the means to pursue extra investment opportunities often took advantage of these.

In 1851 Britain hosted the Great Exhibition of the Works of Industry of All Nations. The event displayed the art, industry, and science that had emerged during the fastest expansion of wealth and the largest increase in economic opportunity that the world had ever seen. The Industrial Revolution had spurred on these developments.

It also disrupted the traditional hierarchies of the time. Rather than the layers of aristocrats, craftsmen, and labor workers holding together society, there was a strong demand for those who could read and write. Workers were hired to create invoices and contracts. Employees provided a wide range of services, including healthcare and education. The number of clerks skyrocketed in England from 44,000 in 1851 to more than 119,000 in 1871.[99]

This wave continued and branched beyond Britain's borders. In 1820 the middle class represented about 1 percent of the world's entire population. During the following two hundred years, it grew

---

98   Homi Kharas, "Middle-Class Lifestyles Start with $10 per Person and Day," D+C: Development and Cooperation, June 23, 2021, https://www.dandc.eu/en/article/middle-class-expanding-particularly-developing-countries.

99   Homi Kharas, "How a Growing Global Middle Class Could Save the World's Economy," Trend Magazine, July 5, 2016, https://www.pewtrusts.org/en/trend/archive/summer-2016/how-a-growing-global-middle-class-could-save-the-worlds-economy.

to become approximately half of the global community. It spread to Europe and the United States during the twentieth century. It extended into Asia and Latin America. This massive segment supports and sustains the global economy today.[100] Much of this increase can be attributed to technology development.[101]

OPPORTUNITIES FOR THE MIDDLE CLASS

In recent years the inequality of wealth has come to the forefront of economic and social discussions. In 2020, amid the pandemic, the total amount of capital still rose in some areas. In others, including Latin America, it plummeted. In North America the overall wealth increased by $12.4 trillion in 2020. That same year Europe saw a growth of $9.2 trillion. These areas encompassed the majority of the wealth increase. China's capital grew by $4.2 trillion, and the Asia-Pacific region figures (not counting China or India) rose by $4.7 trillion. Latin America performed the worst of all regions. There the total wealth dropped by $1.2 trillion.[102]

Coming out of the pandemic and looking into the upcoming years, the overall global wealth is expected to climb. Low- and middle-income countries will play a vital role in this rise. Though they hold just 33 percent of the world's wealth, they are forecast to be responsible for 42 percent of global growth.[103]

As one region thrives, another does not necessarily suffer. Looking at the middle class in context since its start during the Industrial Revolution, it is evident that the growth of this sector in one location is

---

100   Kharas, "How a Growing."

101   Kharas, "Middle-Class Lifestyles."

102   Anshool Deshmukh, "This Simple Chart Reveals the Distribution of Global Wealth," Visual Capitalist, September 20, 2021, https://www.visualcapitalist.com/distribution-of-global-wealth-chart/.

103   Deshmukh, "Simple Chart Reveals."

often associated with more opportunities for citizens in other areas. The Marshall Plan in Europe, for instance, came into effect in 1948. It outlined ways that the United States would help restore the economic infrastructure in Europe after World War II. It aided the middle class in both Europe and the United States.[104]

A growing income segment provides an increased measure of purchasing power. Companies that sell healthcare products to wage earners have a larger market if more people have higher salaries. The same is true for insurance, higher education, and other services. Trade rises alongside a growing middle class.

Collectively the middle-class segment shares values of a strong work ethic, thrift, and individual responsibility.[105] Households in this category make economic-based decisions. While they participate in material consumption, they also look for ways to enjoy life, appreciate art, and participate in leisure activities.

Continued technology advancements create a promising outlook for a growing middle class. Historically developments are first available to the wealthy. Over time they sprinkle into other segments of society. Take the case of electricity. After its invention only the wealthy had access to it. Today electricity is commonplace in middle-income homes around the world. It is part of the middle-class lifestyle.

> *Continued technology advancements create a promising outlook for a growing middle class.*

While it can be easy to idealize the qualities of the middle class, there are potential downsides attached to this segment. As income

104 National Archives, "Marshall Plan (1948)," accessed October 13, 2022, https://www.archives.gov/milestone-documents/marshall-plan.

105 Kharas, "Middle-Class Lifestyles."

levels rise, households consume more. They purchase more food, goods, and services. They use higher amounts of energy. This type of lifestyle can lead to larger quantities of trash. It could be noted, then, that a rise of the middle class brings on concerns related to carbon emissions and waste.

At the same time, families with higher salaries tend to live in urban areas. They are smaller in size too. This is often attributed to more access to education, including girls that finish college and go on to have a career. With higher education rates come stronger employment percentages and fewer children. There also tends to be a growing concern over the environment. This often leads to recycling or contributions to charities that promote sustainability. In this way a growing middle-class segment can play a role in preserving the planet and working to achieve the UN's listed SDGs.[106]

Trends in Tech

The steep rise of cloud technologies, automation, and remote work has rippling effects. Dominating the scene is a drumbeat calling for more tech workers. Trends like e-commerce, social media, and online gaming only intensify the demand. With a current global labor shortage in the technology industry, it can be easy to ask, "What lies ahead?"

In the US, there is a ratio of one to five between software developers and jobs.[107] In other words, for every software developer, there are five open positions. How will this gap be filled in the years to come, especially as tech and its related components continue to grow and expand?

---

106 Kharas, "How a Growing."

107 Ana Djurovic, "New Intel—How Many Software Engineers Are There in 2022?" GoRemotely, January 28, 2022, https://goremotely.net/blog/how-many-software-engineers-are-there/.

The challenge is real, and it's being recognized. The largest hindrance to the adoption of 64 percent of emerging technologies is the talent scarcity, according to IT executives surveying their industry.[108] Companies in nearly every sector are short-staffed in the tech department.

TRAINING TECH EXPERTS

As managers look to hire tech workers, there is oftentimes a disconnect. Executives might search for candidates that have advanced degrees and a long list of skills. The position they're trying to fill might not require an extensive training base. Or managers may be overlooking creative opportunities. For instance perhaps a highly skilled tech professional could supervise a group of employees that have some tech knowledge and are learning as they work.

There can be significant advantages that come from hiring entry-level tech workers or those with midrange skills. First and foremost these positions usually require lower salaries. This provides a cost savings to a company, which can help reduce total operating costs. There is also a chance to train these workers to fit unique roles within the company. If employees receive on-the-job training, they can adapt to the needs of the organization. Finally, with tech advancing so quickly, there is a risk associated with solely hiring college graduates. The courses these workers took during their early years of schooling may no longer apply when they enter the field. Due to this fast outdating of skills, taking on workers that have interest and potential could be an ideal solution. Companies will spend less while simultane-

108 Gartner, "Gartner Survey Reveals Talent Shortages as Biggest Barrier to Emerging Technologies Adoption," September 13, 2021, https://www.gartner.com/en/newsroom/press-releases/2021-09-13-gartner-survey-reveals-talent-shortages-as-biggest-barrier-to-emerging-technologies-adoption.

ously getting the staff they want, along with the adaptiveness required in today's changing tech world.

REMOTE WORK CONCERNS

In recent times the concept of location has taken on new meaning. As the pandemic entered the world, remote working became the norm. Equipped with the ability to digitally connect, workers don't have to be in one city. Thus the talent pool for many industries extends beyond borders. Given this, at first glance it may seem that hiring tech workers in developing nations can provide additional savings for companies. These employees typically receive a lower salary than those in a developed country. They could still maintain a standard of living that is comparable to that of tech workers in first-world regions.

Still there are two main barriers that often prevent established companies from hiring remote talent in developing countries. The first hurdle consists of internet interruptions. If a corporation in a developed society hires a remote worker in a low-income nation, there is frequently a connectivity concern. The employee might live in an area that has unstable infrastructure, sporadic blackouts, or power shortages. Even when connected the worker might not have a strong enough signal or bandwidth to support video conferencing or streaming. This challenge makes it difficult to have a reliable connection. It could cause delays in projects and deadlines. Ultimately a company might even consider the hired position to be a loss, especially if disruptions slow processes or lead to customer complaints.

The second reason that companies hesitate to hire tech talent in developing nations revolves around data security. If a worker has an unsecure connection, others could tap into privately held information. Hackers or scammers might take important data and use it—or threaten to deploy it—against the company. It is often hard for developing countries to provide secure connections. Even if they are available, the employee may not have access to them. Instead the tech worker could be logging in to work at a place with public access to free or low-cost Wi-Fi. In these cases the company is at risk of losing money. While it may be less costly to hire a remote tech worker in a developing nation, if there is a data breach, the end price could be steep and override any initial outsourcing savings.

Thus individuals who live in low-income countries and are interested in a tech-related career face few opportunities. They may not be able to move to a developed nation for work. With limited connectivity and security concerns, there could be few chances of getting hired for remote work by an international company. They might not have access to the higher levels of training and networking needed to get a tech job in their own country.

PROVIDING TECH SOLUTIONS

Despite the obstacles of connecting the developing world to the developed world, the demand for digital and data services continues to grow. Due to the expansion of cloud technology and software, along with AI and machine learning, tech is seeping into nearly every industry. Segments ranging from financial services to healthcare, education, retail, and law are looking for tech support. The same is true for telecom, media, life sciences, and energy sectors. Even those you might not immediately associate with tech, such as agriculture and hospitality, are growing in their use of digital tools.

If established corporations don't hire workers from low-income countries, they are missing out on an available labor pool. The key to making the correlation possible lies in overcoming barriers and creating win-win situations. A reliable, secure internet connection must be available. Staff members from developing countries need to have access to training to develop and uplevel their skills. Once these objectives are achieved, strong connections can develop between international companies and the low-income workforce.

The Future of Work

Coupling the trends in digital solutions with the benefits that a middle class brings, it can be observed that there is ample opportunity for tech work in places like Honduras. Employees that are given the chance to increase their skill set and move to a higher class will likely be motivated. For many it is difficult—if not impossible—to pay for their own training. As such, if teaching programs are provided in a reliable and secure setting, a door is opened. The worker will feel valued and see that an investment has been made in them. They will likely take their role and work assignments very seriously.

That's exactly the thrill that ALTIATEK, located at Altia in San Pedro Sula, provides. Workers who are hired at ALTIATEK receive all the training they need. They can develop their knowledge by accessing world-class online training platforms. They can learn through SkillNow, an onsite training campus, as well as in-person immersive teaching sessions. Experienced staff from around the globe are part of ALTIATEK's makeup. Their presence provides further support for hires who are learning skills and developing their tech careers.

ALTIATEK operates on a full-service model for international companies. It provides partnering services such as customer service management (CSM), IT service management (ITSM), IT operations management (ITOM), and IT asset management (ITAM). It also has cloud services including cloud migration discovery and assessment, cloud migration strategy, cloud migration implementation, and cloud operations. ALTIATEK offers full stack and web development managed services and data science managed services too.

The full-service model solves the main struggles related to stable web connections and data security. In addition to well-trained staff, ALTIATEK provides plug and play workspace for international corporations. This includes personalized office spaces at Altia, cable infrastructure, secure computers and firewalls, and all other services needed to ensure a seamless workflow in a safe and secure environment.

Setting ALTIATEK apart from others in the space is the high-performance team model. Under this structure highly skilled tech professionals oversee small groups of trained staff. These teams are supervised by an experienced management team. The result is a one-stop, all-inclusive solution for global companies with growing tech needs.

THE BENEFITS OF OUTSOURCING IT

Organizations looking to fill tech needs don't necessarily have to create in-house training centers. It's possible to take advantage of the global talent pool and draw from places like ALTIATEK that already have systems in place. There are many advantages that outsourcing tech can bring:

- Time savings: Supervisors don't need to spend hours sorting through applications and conducting interviews. By working with ALTIATEK, the solutions and positions can be provided based on a company's specific needs.

- Cost reductions: Rather than hiring highly trained workers that come with their own set of expectations, drawing from developing nations provides dual benefits. Workers looking to move from low to middle income will see the job as an opportunity to uplevel their skills and future. Companies seeking ways to reduce costs can avoid hiring workers that require $150,000 a year or more. Instead they can onboard an employee with similar or developing skills at a much lower expense.

- Automatic updates: There's no need to constantly retrain staff or upgrade systems when the right outsourcing team is at work. ALTIATEK may agree to take care of all software updates for a product or service as they arise. This alleviates stress for the organization. Managers and executives can direct their time to other high-level tasks that need attention.

- Twenty-four seven support: With the ability to be online at any time, customers are growing to expect instant response time. For time-sensitive tasks, having a team that is in place and operates around the clock can cover ongoing requests. When contracts are drafted to include 24-7 support, there is often peace of mind. Firms can be assured that systems will remain running all the time.

BUILDING UP HONDURAS AND BEYOND

When GK first entered Honduras, it set up factories and hired local workers. These institutions aligned with textile and manufacturing opportunities in the area. The facilities also provided a mechanism for those living in extreme poverty to move into a new way of life. By getting a job, they could enjoy a steady salary. They could provide for their households and not have to worry about finding food every day.

As a country Honduras benefited from higher levels of employment. The increase in jobs also helped reduce migration trends among young people. Employees who spend their days in a working environment are less likely to find themselves on the streets. They have a lower risk of getting wrapped up in the activities of a gang or criminal group.

While all of this could be labeled as success, the vision of GK didn't stop there. Getting out of poverty could be called the first step. What is the second? How about the third? What can be done to collectively pursue the UN's SDGs?

These were the questions GK delved into as the manufacturing facilities, and then Altia, grew and flourished. A search for answers led to droves of new ideas. These are all aimed at helping society take another step forward. After moving from poverty to low income, the next phase could consist of a shift from low-income to middle-income households.

In Honduras only 10 percent of the population is considered middle class. Helping to build wealth could produce long-term benefits for society. Specifically it would generate stronger economic growth and greater social stability. This could lead to lower levels of violence, reductions in crime, and stronger family units.[109]

Members of the middle class in Honduras are reported to make between ten dollars and fifty dollars a day.[110] The makeup of society mirrors other countries in Latin America. Their structure resembles a triangle. The majority live in poverty, forming the lower section of the triangle. Above this class, the middle sector has a small portion. In the tip are the wealthy. This class, though few in number, has the most wealth, control, and power.

Historically it has been difficult for the middle class of Honduras to grow. In the 1950s the portion of middle-income earners increased slightly, spurred on by foreign investment. Middle-income households could afford to pay for higher education for their children. Workers

109 Camden Gilreath, "The Outlook of Poverty in Honduras," The Borgen Project, July 6, 2020, https://borgenproject.org/tag/poverty-in-honduras.

110 Trading Economics, "Honduras—Middle Class," accessed October 14, 2022, https://tradingeconomics.com/honduras/middle-class-$10-50-a-day-headcount-wb-data.html.

found positions as professionals, farmers, merchants, businesses, and civil servants.[111]

When the country went through an economic crisis in the 1980s, the middle class suffered. Many lost their jobs, and some households fell into poverty. Employment opportunities remained scarce during the subsequent years.

The middle-class segment began to experience growth again in the 1990s. During the early years of that decade, basic textile jobs appeared in the country. Toward the late 1990s and early 2000s, the automotive industry gained traction in Honduras. This led to a demand for workers with a higher skill set. While the working class increased, there was still a large potential for further development—and even a boom.

Thus the growing demand in tech could generate a strong supply of jobs in places like Honduras. ALTIATEK in Altia provides the services that international companies need. Employees can use the training to jump-start a career. Society, in turn, can benefit from a dwindling poor class. Its departure gives way for a growing engine—the middle-income segment—and all the economic splendor it brings.

HOW TO DO BUSINESS IN DEVELOPING COUNTRIES

- Start by filling your own company's tech needs. Then evaluate if you could provide services to other firms. What competitive edge could you bring to the market?

- Understand the society of the area in which you operate. Get a grasp of how segments are divided. While developing countries typically have a high low-income population, check the makeup of middle- and high-income sectors.

---

111   US Library of Congress, "Honduras: The Middle Class."Country Studies, accessed October 14, 2022, http://countrystudies.us/honduras/45.htm.

- Talk to team members about how to elevate the middle class in the country of operations. Ask them what benefits they would like to see. Discuss how a growing middle class could impact their country.

- When deciding on wages, research what middle earners make in the developing country you are interested in. Think about what you could offer. You might be able to include a higher-than-normal paycheck, along with tech skills training.

CHAPTER 10

Build a Green Future

Survey the pulse of Green Valley Manufacturing Hub on any given day, and you'll notice two lines of work. One takes place at an interior level. The other occurs in the exterior—specifically outdoors. At the industrial hub in Santa Barbara, Honduras, what goes on in both places is equally important.

Inside you'll find laborers hard at work. Their skills produce goods that will be sent from the factories to different parts of the world. Their efforts focus on the textile, automotive, life sciences, and food processing industries. The role of employees is essential. Without them Green Valley wouldn't exist.

The same is true for what goes on in the open air of the hub. Here the motivation shifts from the quota-driven manufacturing schedules to the landscape of tomorrow. Outdoors the focus is on preservation, and its activities are future driven. Through the practices that take place on the fields of Green Valley come job security for the plant's workers, along with clean air for their families to breathe.

During the week you'll find workers in the garden and nursery of the manufacturing hub. They plant new seeds and cultivate flowers, herbs, and decorative bushes. They transport food scraps from the buildings of the hub to the compost pile. There they mix the organic material into the soil and apply the Bokashi method.

This type of composting was first developed in the 1980s by Dr. Teuro Higa, a professor at the University of Ryukyus in Okinawa, Japan. It quickly spread throughout Asia to ferment food. The method only takes about ten days to complete. The nutrient value of the material produced is among the highest of all composting results. It uses special equipment and materials to break down organic food waste, including fruits, vegetables, meat, dairy, and fats.[112]

To carry out the method, food scraps are layered and mixed with an inoculant that consists of wheat germ, wheat bran or sawdust mixed with molasses, and effective microorganisms. The microorganisms consume the wheat germ, bran, or sawdust mixture. After about ten days, the material can be shifted to another place to finish decomposing.[113]

At Green Valley, state-of-the-art infrastructure is infused with an environmental management system.

The Bokashi method has several key advantages. First it allows dairy and meat scraps to be used in the compost process. These two materials are traditionally left out of other decomposing methods. It produces a highly nutritious plant food and can be used as a fertilizer. It is also useful for vermicomposting, a process in which earthworms break down waste and create a natural, organic fertilizer. Both methods—the Bokashi and vermicomposting—take place on a continual basis at Green Valley.

112   Colleen Vanderlinden, "The Basics of Bokashi Composting: A Composting Method Using Fermentation," The Spruce, July 12, 2022, https://www.thespruce.com/basics-of-bokashi-composting-2539742.

113   Vanderlinden, "Basics of Bokashi."

Every month the Bokashi method produces one ton of fertilizer at the industrial hub. The material is redistributed throughout the grounds. It is directed to plant growth and development along the boulevards of Green Valley. It adorns the lawns surrounding the factory buildings. It is also used in reforestation efforts in nearby areas.

At Green Valley, state-of-the-art infrastructure is infused with an environmental management system. It has the largest industrial solar plant in Central America and the most competitive electricity cost in the region. Its 100 percent recyclable water treatment center and carbon-neutral strategies serve as testimony to its commitment to sustainability. Composting materials is a key component of this intricate system.

At GK we aim to positively contribute toward the UN's SDGs. And you can too. Creating a green tomorrow is a task that requires research and analysis. It embraces innovation and renewable resources.

In the following sections, we'll review the development of clean energy. We'll look at the benefits renewables provide to forward-looking, mindful companies. We'll spend some time thinking about what type of planet the next generation will inherit. I recommend that you keep the information and ideas in mind as you work to build your own green future.

The History of Energy

Civilizations of centuries past relied on firewood for energy. When burned, wood produced heat. The method was used to keep homes and buildings warm during cold months. However, its thermal energy wasn't converted to other uses.

The invention of the steam engine during the eighteenth century brought swift change. It forever altered the world's landscape. The steam engine debuted a way that the heat from wood could be used as a source of power. Its presence ushered in the Industrial Revolution and mass production.

The invention also provided a growing demand for wood and later coal. The Coal Age began in 1920, when the resource accounted for 62 percent of energy consumption. Petroleum then entered the scene, shifting coal aside and leading the world into a new era. In 1965 petroleum held the top spot for energy production. Just as the steam engine and coal created a revolution, oil and gas did the same.[114]

While these resources certainly led to advancements for society, they have also presented steep drawbacks. Environmental pollution has skyrocketed. An industrialized world continues to produce carbon emissions. Fossil fuels are not renewable. Their supply is finite. The logistics chain connecting the source of fuels to their destination is fragile too. Disruptions lead to higher prices for consumers and companies. Uncertainty about the future abounds.

The Renewables Revolution

During the past decades, the emergence of renewable sources has created a solution to these environmental issues. Thanks to recent advances, green resources hold the power to ignite another revolution. This one, however, will be hallmarked by energy efficiency, carbon-neutral processes, and human development around the world.

Through this new revolution, the power supply system will shift from energy plants to individual homes and buildings. That's because solar energy can be produced at a micro level and then shared through a grid. A school, for instance, could generate its own power

---

114   Gao Jifan, "The Next Energy Revolution Is Already Here," World Economic Forum, September 20, 2017, https://www.weforum.org/agenda/2017/09/next-energy-revolution-already-here.

supply through roof panels that absorb the sun's rays and turn them into electricity. If more power is produced than the school needs, it can share the excess via the grid. During summer months when the education building is hardly used, the energy could be sent to a nearby grocery store. Arrangements such as this already exist in places like Germany, where households are equipped with rooftop panels. If one home generates more energy than the residing family uses, the power is shifted to the regional grid, where it can be accessed by others in need.[115]

The renewables revolution could further break down barriers to energy, especially among the world's poor. In places where communities do not have access to electricity, there may be no need to build in power lines. Instead solar panels could be delivered to homes. Through these, households could receive electricity for the first time. After the initial investment has been paid, the cost to soak up the sun's rays is minimal or nothing at all.

INVESTING IN RENEWABLE ENERGY

For decades investments in fossil fuel production provided jobs for both blue-collar and white-collar workers. In recent years advances in renewable energy have led to more employment opportunities. In 2018 the renewable energy sector provided eleven million jobs. In 2019 that number grew to 11.5 million.[116]

The trend continues today. An investment in solar-photovoltaic equipment creates 1.5 times as many jobs as the same amount placed on fossil fuel production. (Solar photovoltaic initiatives convert energy

---

115   Jifan, "Next Energy Revolution."

116   Roli Srivastava, "How to Tackle Covid-19 Jobs Crisis and Climate Change? Invest in Clean Energy," World Economic Forum, October 21, 2021, https://www.weforum.org/agenda/2021/10/the-strong-benefits-of-renewable-energy.

directly to electricity.) For wind power 1.2 times the number of jobs are developed for each investment compared to fossil fuel processes.[117] Workers who previously participated in gas and oil production could be retrained to work in solar or wind sectors. The growth in jobs also provides an opportunity to bring more workers into the renewable industry.

During recent years costs related to produce renewable energy have fallen. From 2010 to 2019, expenses tied to solar photovoltaics projects dropped by 82 percent. Costs associated with onshore wind initiatives declined by 39 percent. The drops can be attributed to better technologies, the scaling of production, and more experienced developers. The result is that green projects are now more cost effective than coal-fired power plants.[118]

Opportunities for a Renewable World

At GK we hold a vision for a planet that operates on renewable resources. And we are not alone. It is possible to switch to a fully sustainable global energy system within the next thirty years, according to research gathered by Stanford University.

One component of this endeavor could consist of a super grid connecting North America. This renewable structure would tie together the regions of the US, Canada, and Mexico. It would reduce the need to store energy and lower the overall production and distribution costs.[119]

---

117 Srivastava, "How to Tackle."

118 Harry Kretchmer, "The Cost of Renewable Energy Is Increasingly Undercutting Fossils," World Economic Forum, June 23, 2020, https://www.weforum.org/agenda/2020/06/cost-renewable-energy-cheaper-coal.

119 Johnny Wood, "Renewable Energy Could Power the World by 2050. Here's What that Future Might Look Like," World Economic Forum, February 28, 2020, https://www.weforum.org/agenda/2020/02/renewable-energy-future-carbon-emissions.

Besides the opportunities for efficiency, there is a quality-of-life component tied to renewables. From a health standpoint, the current energy supply puts lives at risk. Populations in urban areas awake to skies of smog every morning. Switching to the power of wind, water, and solar leads to cleaner air. Using these resources, rather than oil and coal, could reduce the number of deaths related to air pollution. Specifically, between four to seven million lives would be saved annually by using renewables.[120]

INVESTING IN RENEWABLE ENERGY

Since GK started in Honduras and expanded into other regions, it has maintained a focus on renewable energy. One of the initial reasons for this stemmed from the desire to be independent from government-supplied resources. This approach is different from the method used by many companies that invest in developing countries. It is common to work with governments to set up initial infrastructure and utilities. While GK has always been open to collaborating, there are limitations that come with depending on energy. For instance if an energy system crashes, the company can be left without power. In developing nations power outages are common. In some places households even schedule their days around the power supply. If

One of the initial reasons for our focus on renewable energy stemmed from the desire to be independent from government-supplied resources.

a sector generally doesn't have electricity in the evenings, homes with a washing machine will often run it during the morning hours.

---

120 Wood, "Renewable Energy."

Manufacturing hubs with deadlines to meet and contracts in place cannot afford to start and stop production intermittently. As such, GK has always sought ways to be energy independent. Taking on the responsibility that comes with being a global company, we have also looked for sustainable resources. The benefits here are multifold. There are cost reductions that come with relying on renewable energy. These efficiencies can be passed on to companies that are using the facilities. It is also advantageous for companies that want to invest and have stakeholders with environmental priorities.

In a world that is becoming increasingly focused on green initiatives, operating in a place that provides renewable energy eases a company's environmental concerns. This trend will likely intensify in the years to come. This is due, in large part, to increased pressure on global organizations to reduce their carbon footprints.

For companies that are looking to invest in renewable energy strategies, the starting point is often an assessment of current use. As they say, "If you can't measure it, you can't improve it." Thus an organization needs to evaluate how much energy is being consumed. This includes a look at electricity expenditures, utility costs, water bills, and so on. Once the numbers are in, they can be used as a basis. An organization may decide to track certain metrics and report the figures every month, every quarter, or every year. The best practices will depend on its industry and the interests of its stakeholders.

When searching for ways to reduce energy consumption and costs, there are often certain roadblocks to break down. This could involve location, such as a manufacturing facility located in an area that doesn't provide renewable resources. It might be related to rising costs of electricity in a region. Once an organization has identified the challenge, it can explore possibilities for improvement. It could shift operations to a location that has more renewable energy resources available. It may purchase equipment that uses less electricity and provides a higher return on investment. It could reuse materials or sell byproduct from processes rather than throw it away.

BEST PRACTICES ALWAYS WIN

The focus on reducing waste may be making the headlines more consistently. The concept, however, has long existed in the business world. Before the acronym CSR (corporate social responsibility) surfaced, there was a tendency to use these principles, according to Bob Humphrey, CEO of Delta Apparel, an apparel company based in Duluth, Georgia, with operations in Central America. During his initial years in the business, Bob learned from leaders who looked for ways to carry out CSR. He went on to follow in their steps, with an eye for continual improvement.

Whenever a garment is produced, there is waste involved. Fabric is cut, and the remnants remain. However, the leftover material doesn't need to be thrown out. White scraps might be separated from the others and then sold. It could go on to have a second life as stuffing. Other portions of waste from apparel production can be used to make mock yarn.

While CSR has always been important, a growing number of companies have started to publicly document their processes. Corporate renewable procurement has grown by 60 percent during the last ten years. Still there is much to be done, especially to reach the UN's targets in the coming years.[121]

---

121 Chris Gunsten, "The Pros and Cons of Investing in Renewable Energy Supply Chains," Loyola University Chicago Supply Chain and Sustainability Center, https://www.luc.edu/supplychaincenter/insights/articlesandpublications/renewableenerg-yandthesupplychainsoftomorrow.shtml.

The world's energy supply is undergoing a transformation. At the heart of this change lies a chance to improve the lives of everyone. Leaning on renewable resources produces better air and supports good health for citizens. These energy sources are more accessible to all people. Opting for wind and solar power also reduces the amount of carbon emissions released every year.

The planet is well positioned for an energy revolution. At GK we're ready and equipped to lead the way. As you look ahead, I invite you to join in the campaign. Keep green at the forefront of your long-term investments. You'll be able to reduce costs and serve as an example for others to follow.

HOW TO DO BUSINESS IN DEVELOPING COUNTRIES

- Before implementing a green project, weigh the costs and benefits. Beyond the up-front investment, consider the long-term return. Create a system to monitor the savings it brings over time.

- Pay attention to upcoming renewable solutions. Trends in clean energy continue to evolve, and prices may further reduce in the coming years.

- Look for ways to generate power without relying on other sources such as the local infrastructure.

- When carrying out humanitarian aid, keep solar in mind. You may be able to help impoverished areas gain access to power for little cost.

CHAPTER 11

Make a Multiplying Effect

George Soros, a Hungarian-born businessman and philanthropist, listened to stories of World War I as a child. His father had spent time in Siberia during the Russian Revolution of 1917. He shared tales of his past with George as they exercised in the swimming pool after school hours.[122]

The experiences left an impression on George. So did the coming years. In 1944 when Nazi Germany occupied Hungary, George was thirteen years old. As part of a Jewish family, George's life was suddenly in danger. The Nazi authorities started deporting Jews to extermination camps.

George watched his father, a lawyer who understood the nature of the Nazi regime, work to arrange false identity papers. These were given to their family and friends. His father also organized hiding places for them. Most of the people he tried to help survived.

Collectively this time of George's life would forever impact his views on the world, democracy, and human rights. When the Nazi regime retreated, the Soviet Union occupied Hungary. George took refuge in England, where he studied at the London School of Economics. He went on to become a hedge manager and grew heavily

---

122 George Soros, *In Defense of Open Society* (New York: Hachette Book Group, 2019).

involved in the financial markets. Over time he accumulated massive amounts of wealth. The level of success he reached gave him pause. He reflected on life and his priorities. He realized he was most passionate about open society and helping individuals gain freedom and individual rights.

As a result he established the Open Society in 1979. Its first initiative sought ways to weaken the apartheid system in South Africa. It provided scholarships for Black African university students there. The foundation later aided the opening of the Soviet system. It expanded into different countries during the following decades. It grew to become the largest private human rights funder, with investments totaling over $18 billion toward causes including democracy, economic equity, education, health, and antidiscrimination.[123]

George's story relates how experiences in our lives affect our business decisions. As you work in a developing country, you'll come across specific challenges. To create lasting change, it's vital to overcome these obstacles. Strategies for solutions can be written into your business plan.

> *The best approach includes maintaining integrity at every step.*

The best approach includes maintaining integrity at every step. It also involves collaborating with other organizations that share your firm's values. Caring for workers is the final component to instill a culture that seeks positive change.

We'll look at each of these in turn. As you read, think about the values you want for your own organization. Consider how to incorporate the changes you want to make to society into your business

---

123   Open Society Foundations, "Who We Are," accessed October 15, 2022, https://www.opensocietyfoundations.org/who-we-are.

goals. Don't underestimate the importance of culture. When workers feel appreciated and have a chance to grow, they're more likely to contribute toward the organization's established objectives.

Ethics at Every Turn

Setting an elevated bar enables GK to maneuver the legal landscape of developing countries. Fragile economies throughout much of the world operate in a system with distinct order. In developed countries it is considered common practice to have an established rule of law. Nations with low levels of infrastructure typically favor the elite. Common workers may be subject to the law. Those of high rank could be exempt.

Banks and lenders in developing countries may consider themselves above the law. If a firm takes out a loan and misses even a single payment, the financial institution overseeing the installment schedule might have the right to overtake the organization. The lender may not have to face any charges, even if the establishment is accused of wrongdoing.

In developing and developed countries alike, the connectivity of the internet and media outlets can pose risks for businesses that want to do good. Stories that paint a company in a poor light can go viral. The information portrayed may not be true. If it is sensational, viewers will likely click and read. Those in positions of authority could leverage their power and twist the reputation of a firm. Officials might tear down a company's brand for their own political gain.

At various points throughout its years of operation, GK has faced scrutiny. Legal issues have surfaced. Fake news headlines have accused the company of foul play. By and large our team has maintained integrity in all circumstances. Remaining truthful ultimately prevails.

Supporting the Ruth Paz Foundation

Based in San Pedro Sula, the Ruth Paz Foundation is a nonprofit that provides medical services to low-income children. It offers general and specialized surgeries, carried out by local surgeons and US surgical brigades. These operations treat issues related to hernias, the gallbladder, cysts, cleft lip and palate, cardiac, and scoliosis, among others. The medical center maintained by the Ruth Paz Foundation is the only burn unit in Honduras that gives comprehensive care. It serves more than forty-two thousand people a year and conducts over 1,800 surgeries.[124]

The founder of the organization, Ruth Paz, was originally from the United States. She moved from Detroit, Michigan, to Honduras and grew passionate about helping the poor in the 1960s. Her heart went out to little ones who were sick or handicapped and couldn't afford to get medical treatment. One of her first activities involved bringing in Donald Laub, a professor at Stanford University and the founder of Interplast, an organization dedicated to helping lives through plastic and reconstructive surgery in underprivileged areas. Dr. Laub came with his team to San Pedro Sula. They operated on children with congenital defects.

Ruth devoted the remainder of her life to helping children in Honduras. She took severely burned young ones to the US for medical treatment. She continued to work with US surgeons and dreamed of opening a clinic that would provide dentistry and orthodontic care for children who needed treatment after cleft lip and palate surgery.

Ruth passed away in 1996. At that time her family continued to carry on her legacy. Her daughter, Mary Ann de Kafati, stepped into

---

124 Ruth Paz Foundation, "About Us," accessed October 15, 2022, https://en.fundacionruthpaz.org/quienes-somos.

the role of president. She oversaw the opening of the Ruth Paz Clinic in 1997, fulfilling the wishes of her mother to provide pediatric dental services. "Growing up, there were often children in our home," Mary Ann recalled. "My mother would keep them with us until she could take them to the US for treatment." Being raised in this environment shaped her view of the world. "Being poor does not mean it's okay to lack healthcare access ... or to receive care in precarious and overcrowded conditions where the risk of hospital acquired infections threaten the lives of children," she shared.[125]

Today the hospital run by the Ruth Paz Foundation is one of the only facilities in the country that provides high-quality specialty care for children. Services and medications are distributed for free or at low cost, based on the individual's financial need. Patients with first- and second-degree burns are treated at the hospital. Those with third-degree burns are taken by air ambulance to hospitals in the US.

The treatment a patient receives at the hospital can be lifesaving. It also helps individuals avoid the financial consequences that often come with an accident or defect. A child born with a cleft lip and palate, for instance, may get ridiculed in school. The result could lower their motivation to continue with their studies and decrease their chance of employment. For workers a condition that requires them to step away from their job could lead to unemployment.

Such was the case for Franklin Lopez, a nineteen-year-old who broke his femur in a motorcycle accident in 2019. He spent the next twenty-one days at home, without receiving proper care. His mother then pooled her resources and took him to the Ruth Paz Foundation hospital. The family lived about sixty miles from the facility, and the

---

125 Ruth Paz Foundation, "About Us."

trip there drained their meager cash supply. When Franklin arrived he received surgery for his leg.[126]

Two days later he was discharged from the hospital. However, his family now faced another crisis. They had no funds left for the trip home. Moreover he couldn't take a bus with his limited mobility. A private car would cost $160, an amount the family did not have. At the hospital they connected with another patient's family who lived near them. The family was returning home in a car, and Franklin and his mother were able to ride with them.[127]

For others facing circumstances like Franklin, the foundation covers the cost of transportation. More importantly it gives them hope for the future. After healing, Franklin would be eligible to return to the workforce. Without proper treatment that may not have been possible.

GK supports the Ruth Paz Foundation, collaborating as one of its donors so it can continue to serve the children of Honduras. "Whenever I ask, they never turn me away," shared Mary Ann, referring to her requests to GK Foundation for aid. While she notes that raising funding can be difficult in a poverty-stricken country, she also believes in the mission and wants to carry out her mother's legacy. With supporters such as GK and others, Ruth Paz Foundation can continue its tireless work to raise a healthier generation of children in Honduras.

Collaborating with Nonprofits

GK Foundation works with other organizations too. The efforts are not always highly advertised. "I would rather take resources and put

---

126 Francesca Volpi, "With Few Options for Care, Families in Honduras Journey to Ruth Paz Foundation Hospital," Direct Relief, February 23, 2019, https://www.directrelief. org/2019/02/families-honduras-ruth-paz-foundation-hospital/.

127 Volpi, "With Few Options."

them toward the needs of the people," explained Georgina Barahona, director of GK corporate affairs and GK Foundation. "If I have $600, I'm going to use that toward medical supplies and not a shiny advertisement page on a flyer."

Through initiatives like the Amar y Compartir clinic in Honduras and the UHI Clinic in the United States, GK is reaching people around the world. The efforts of ChildLife Foundation have resulted in saving 1.5 million lives of children each year. Every day, families that need healthcare and feel without hope receive treatment and medicine. They also interact with a medical staff that prioritizes dignity, regardless of a family's economic condition. Every patient is shown that their life has value.

It is evident that higher numbers of people can be impacted when collaborations occur. Much like George Soros wanted to assist millions and extend aid as far as possible, GK Foundation has a mission to help as many as it can. By pooling resources more facilities can be built in Honduras, Central America, Asia, and beyond.

Every Worker Matters

GK holds its employees in high esteem. It maintains a family-like culture in all its operations. Our firm is designed to help workers improve their skills. They have a chance to uplevel their lives too. Here's a sampling of some of the positive changes GK workers have undergone.

GETTING A HOME

Esther Benitez Gomez joined GK in Campeche over ten years ago. She grew up in a small village called Palizada, located more than three hundred kilometers from the city of Campeche. She would have stayed there, except for one problem. As an adult she had a baby to feed. There was no work available in the village.

The situation led her to the city of Campeche, where she hoped to find employment opportunities. She came upon GK. There she applied for a position in one of the textile plants at its industrial hub. "I was so nervous at the interview and was certain they wouldn't give me a job," she recalled. "I didn't know anything about sewing."

To Esther's surprise she was hired and given training for the job. Once she became familiar with the work, she was promoted to a more complex machine. The new equipment was all-purpose. Using it enabled her to expand her skill set.

"At every step I came across leaders in the factory that encouraged me and helped me learn how to best do my job," Esther said. Eager to advance, Esther took on each new task and worked to master it. Her efforts paid off: she was given a role as trainer to teach new hires how to carry out basic duties.

In addition to a paycheck and promotion, Esther found a group at GK that supported her as a person. "They gave me time off to go to parent meetings at my child's school," she explained. (This practice of giving hours off is often not available in factories in developing countries—GK is an exception.) She was also able to schedule appointments at the company's on-site medical facility. "I love that they help me and others get preventative care from the doctor and have systems in place so that medical costs are not excessive for workers," she added. Over time Esther received the credits needed to purchase her own home. This was a dream come true for her and her family.

Esther's story doesn't end there. "I'm so happy for the opportunity that GK has given me to work and develop a passion for my craft," she stated. "In addition to my house, my son has been able to study and finish his studies at the university level. He now has a degree in business and finance. And I know I'm not alone. Many others at GK have been given the chance to grow and succeed too."

BUILDING A FUTURE

When Laura Hernan de Gonzalez began to work as a seamstress at GK in Campeche, she had no idea what the future would bring. She knew she had to support her family, which consisted of two children. She had a desire to work hard to make it happen. She soon mastered the basics and was promoted to supervisor. "When I moved up, I received a lot of recognitions, including an invitation to have lunch with my boss in his office," she recollected.

Though she was at one time worried about how she would provide for her children, Laura found that GK gave her economic and moral support. "My two treasures grew up and were able to study nursing and law," she explained. "At GK I found a family, and I am forever grateful for that."

A CAREER WITHOUT LIMITS

Antonio Zamora was hired at GK in Campeche more than two decades ago. "I started as a textile machine operator," he stated. "After about three years, I was promoted to be an instructor; then I became a supervisor." A few years later, Antonio moved into a management position in the factory. "I became a production manager, followed by a plant manager, and then director of operations."

Antonio didn't grow up in Campeche. He was born in Tixmucuy, a town about forty kilometers outside of the city. Tixmucuy has a population of just over six hundred people. Job opportunities were very limited. When Antonio heard of possibilities in Campeche, he traveled there and came across GK—where he stayed.

He didn't have a higher education when he started with the company. While working at GK, Antonio completed his college degree, thanks to the company's help and support with his studies. He also purchased a home, where he raised a family. His three children are all studying with the goal of higher levels of education and professional careers.

Reflecting on the last few years, Antonio is thankful for the steadfastness GK has provided. "The pandemic brought hard times, but the company continued to progress," he noted. "Despite massive layoffs by other corporations in the area, the plant has kept its operations running." It also looked out for the health of its workers. "GK donated medical robes and face masks, along with oxygen to its employees as needed," Antonio noted.

Even as routines restarted after the Covid-19 outbreak, GK has continued to play an important role in supporting the health of Campeche's citizens, along with residents in surrounding areas. "When an earthquake struck the nearby state of Oaxaca, GK donated materials and funding to the victims," Antonio stated. The company has also supplied flood victims with food and humanitarian aid.

Cultivating Relationships

Several years ago David Miller, a vice president of sales and marketing for GK based in North Carolina, and I met at the Chicago airport. From there we ventured out on a business trip together. For our first leg, we drove to Kenosha, Wisconsin. In the city we had a meeting with the leadership of an international apparel company. The discussion was very positive. We left on a high note, seeing the promise of future projects on the horizon.

I suggested we celebrate on the way back. After discussing the possibilities, we opted to get a milkshake at McDonald's. While there we stood in line alongside other customers, waiting to place our order. A woman near us admired my shoes and asked where I got them. I thanked her, told her I got them in New York, and asked her where she had purchased hers.

Every component of these interactions is important, from meeting with the retail conglomerate executives to discussing shoes with the fellow customer in line at a fast-food restaurant. Wherever we go, relationships are real.

This core value is firmly embedded into GK culture, and it extends to both team members and beyond. David noticed this shortly after joining the company in 2010. "It intrigued me, during those early years working for GK, that each time I would visit Honduras, by the time I landed in Miami, I would have received a text from Yusuf, thanking me for whatever my purpose was for traveling to San Pedro Sula," he explained.

At first David was impressed by the management technique. "As we developed a more valued friendship, I learned these messages were far more," he stated. "They were a reflection of a compassionate personality."

The Multiplier Factor

Compassion is exactly what drives us to continue our efforts in society. When carried out well, there is a multiplying effect. Those who have been helped turn and look for ways to give back in their own way.

Such is the case at Casa Hogar, an orphanage outside of Campeche that GK supports. Director Mimi Rebeka Aké Chablé, who oversees the shelter, creates a child-focused environment. Everything carried out within the borders of the complex is directed toward building a better future. Children are given a routine, including being fed at certain times and going to bed at regular hours. They see each other, and the volunteers that help raise them, as one unit. "We are all family here," Mimi iterated.

Through volunteers and donors, the children of the home are given a new chance at life. One girl arrived at the home when she was five years old. The shelter provided everything she needed, from food to clothing and an education. She was able to get a job and leave the shelter as an adult. Still she comes back to help the children at the orphanage. There she is known as "Auntie."[128]

> *Compassion drives our efforts in society. When carried out well, there is a multiplying effect.*

A BETTER FUTURE

George Soros has referred to himself and his philanthropic projects as "a selfish man with a selfless foundation."[129] Though he recognized his limitations, he continued to direct initiatives and fund causes that were close to his heart. George also brought in others to help. In doing so his foundations created a chain of aid that spread across the globe.

While it can be easy to see needs in developing nations, it is not always clear how best to provide help. Working with an experienced organization that understands the deep struggles of poverty can be a first step toward implementing real change. By investing together, lives can be touched, futures can be painted, and hope can be instilled.

At the beginning of the pandemic, Sohail Tabba, cofounder of the ChildLife Foundation, wrote about the effects of isolation. After

---

128 TMC Noticias, "La Gobernadora Layda Elena Sansores San Roman Visito a la Casa Hogar El Palomar," http://tmcnoticias.com/?p=29441.

129 Soros, In Defense of Open.

comparing his confined living quarters to conditions that the elderly often face, he turned his thoughts toward the world's poor:

Dispossessed of the range of activities we have crafted for ourselves, we are beginning to imagine the existential plight of 71 million refugees torn from their homes by war, persecution, and human-rights violations. Feeling deprived in the comfort of our homes, we are gaining greater empathy for the 3 billion people who live on less than $2.50 a day. Thrilled at the sight of birds flying across the clear blue skies, we are evolving regret for the 2,000 species we drive to extinction each year on a planet we are suffocating with our heat, pollution, and filth.[130]

George Soros accumulated wealth. Then he directed his foundations toward bettering societies. He emphasized and circulated his values with others. Like him, at GK we have sought to act ethically in our business practices. We have looked to collaborate with nonprofits. We have improved conditions for workers. In these ways our company strives to paint a brighter future for upcoming generations.

You can too. I invite you to incorporate social strategies into your business plan. Keep a clean record to avoid getting bogged down with legal struggles in developing countries. Then look for other organizations to act as partners. Collectively there are opportunities to do more for society.

HOW TO DO BUSINESS IN DEVELOPING COUNTRIES

- Before entering a developing country, research its legal infrastructure. Find information regarding corruption and unethical practices. Understand how loans work before making a deal.

---

130 Muhammad Sohail Tabba, "From Social Distance to Social Integration," *The Express Tribune*, April 29, 2020, https://tribune.com.pk/story/2209679/social-distance-social-integration.

- Get to know the nonprofits in your area. Collaborate with those who share your values. Invite others to come in once you have established your organization.

- Help workers find ways to improve their lives. This may include learning new skills, getting access to medical care, and having the resources to move into their own home.

CONCLUSION

Not long ago my driver Jairo was transporting my three children and me to a local restaurant in San Pedro Sula. As we entered the parking lot of the eatery, we passed a homeless man. I spotted him at the same time as Jairo. My three children saw him too. I knew my kids were hungry. I couldn't help but wonder if the man was famished too. Given the status of the poor in Honduras, along with his extended hand, I assumed he was in need of a meal.

I asked Jairo to pull over and got out of the vehicle. "Are you hungry?" I asked the man. "When did you last eat?" He said that yes, he had not had food in some time and could use a meal.

We went on to the restaurant. While there I ordered a dish for the homeless man. With the food tucked in a takeaway box, Jairo and I returned to the place we had first seen the person. He was still there. Jairo handed him the food. We added in some cash to help him with his next meal.

When Jairo shares this story with others, he adds that he has looked for ways to help others in his own life. With the salary he earns through GK, he has been able to save money. This was never possible in his previous jobs. He now has enough to think of the future. He has also started building a home for his wife and their daughter. The building has gone up in phases, which is common in developing countries. When money comes in, bricks are purchased.

They are used to build a room. A roof goes on that section, and it is furnished. Then money is tucked away, little by little, until more material can be bought and another room constructed.

Jairo is not alone. His efforts mirror many of his coworkers'. Those who know and participate in the GK Foundation follow the same principles. They dedicate their free time to assisting schools and orphanages. They raise funds to make it possible to bring a daily snack to children and pay teachers a fair wage. Collectively their contributions create a multiplier effect, which can be a powerful tool that changes lives.

I come from a country where the majority live in extreme poverty. I now live in a nation that faces many of the same challenges. There is not a day that goes by in which I am not aware of this. I constantly have reminders—visibly and mentally—of what these people are going through:

- The woman in tattered, mismatched clothing asking for food from the park bench

- The barefoot child walking alongside cars stopped at a red light, hand extended

- The mother cradling an infant in the emergency room of a hospital, head bowed, hoping for help

How will these individuals and their families face tomorrow? One might argue that donating to charities is the best answer. Some successful businesses share significant portions of their revenues each year for certain causes.

It should be noted, however, that these funds do not always stay within the country. A business operating in Argentina might make a significant contribution to a museum in London. While there certainly isn't anything wrong about those efforts, at GK we believe the best place to start is close to home.

Handing out money cannot—in and of itself—significantly change a person's life. Perhaps they will receive food for the day. This is important. It's also only a start. There is more that can be done. Health conditions can be improved, education standards can be raised, and income levels can be increased.

These results are possible if your next business venture and your next investments focus on fragile economies. Efforts that center on a circular economy are based on helping people, the communities where they live, their cities, and their countries. The desire is to uplevel the human living condition and extends beyond singular economic motives.

> *Handing out money cannot—in and of itself—significantly change a person's life. Perhaps they will receive food for the day. This is important. It's also only a start.*

At GK the environment will always play a vital role in all our operations. The model can serve as an example to others. It also demonstrates that sustainability can improve the health of citizens around the world.

Wherever you are, in some way there will be opportunities to help others. It doesn't matter if that aid extends to one person, to a few, or to many. Whatever way it happens, lives can be touched, improved, and impacted in a way that won't be forgotten.

Through it all society collectively climbs out of poverty. People enjoy a higher quality of life. They look to the future and think about the next generation.

And then they, in turn, extend a hand to those in need.

ACKNOWLEDGMENTS

Family is a fundamental pillar for one's success, and my case is no exception. I am deeply thankful for the untiring support of my brothers, Toufique Amdani and Dr. Sultan Amdani. A special thanks to my younger brother, Ashraf Amdani, with whom I work on a day-to-day basis. His disciplined manner of conducting business and larger-than-life heart, which is committed to helping people around the world, consistently shine through. His dedication to family and friends sets an example for all to follow. He has always extended a hand to me, in every aspect of life, ready to work through the next step together. I am also appreciative of my late sister, Shahida Amdani, whose memory remains with us today. Much gratitude is owed to my sisters Razia Amdani and Samina Amdani as well.

In addition I want to recognize my nephew Arshad Amdani, who is CEO of GK's textile division, and my nephews Mohammed Ahmad and Ammar Amdani, who manage our VC firm and our technology division. I think fondly of my extended family in Pakistan, the U.S., Dubai, and the U.K., including my nephews and nieces who live there.

I will always treasure the friendship of my cousin Shoaib Kothawala, who resides in California. He has always been available for advice, support, and anything else needed throughout the years.

Our partner and family member Mr. Sohail Tabba, cofounder of the Child Life Foundation, businessman, and philanthropist, is a true gem in our lives. I am pleased to acknowledge the entire Tabba family and commend them for the charitable work they carry out.

My childhood friend Anwer Jetpurwala went to school with me and welcomed me into his family home on many evenings, where we studied for exams and were graciously served tea and snacks by his late beloved mother. His entire family and our friendship remain dear to me now, and I treasure our memories together.

Mr. Arif Doni has been a friend and part of our family for more than forty years. He has consistently assisted in many charitable efforts and demonstrated support for initiatives to improve conditions in Pakistan. Mr. Anjum Zafar has been an unconditional friend and business partner for more than thirty years.

When I first arrived in California, my roommates and dear friends, Irfan and Arif, welcomed me. They supported me at every stage, which I appreciate to this day. My friend Eric Hoffman accompanied me on my pioneering trip to Honduras. I recall our times together and am grateful that our relationship has lasted for more than thirty years.

During my first visit to Honduras in 1990, I met Mr. Roberto Leiva, who was working at that time as president of the chamber of commerce. Later he became director of Fundharse, a foundation of socially responsible companies, and I continued to work with him. I was honored to preside on the foundation for four years and work hands on with him. To this day I have the highest regard and appreciation for his friendship and support.

On that same initial trip, I encountered Mr. Eduardo Facusse, who had a large woven textile mill in Honduras. I visited his facility, and we became friends; our companionship has endured throughout the decades. We continue to cross paths and enjoy each other's company to this day.

The exploratory trip to Honduras in 1990 resulted in another, equally important, friendship. I met the late Don Juan Canahuati, who at the time was a pioneer in the textile industry and the first industrial hub developer. He treated me as a son and frequently invited me to his home on the weekends for a meal and to spend time with his family. His sons, Mario, Jesus, Juan Diego, and Edgardo, have carried out his legacy. Today their company, Elcatex Group, is one of the largest textile and industrial hub developers in the region. We developed a strong relationship that has endured for more than three decades. I have profound memories of Don Juan Canahuati and share the same spirit with his family today.

In Honduras Mr. Roberto Bueso grew to be a very dear friend. He provided constant guidance wherever needed and generously offered his support on every occasion. I met Mr. Roberto Morales by way of my first auditing company. Both friends introduced me to the benefits of tennis and golf. More than twenty-five years later, we still meet each week to play a match or round together.

Mr. Luis Larach and his father, Don Napoleon Larach, have become more than family to me in Honduras. In addition to our business interactions, I have enjoyed a personal relationship with them that has lasted for all our years together.

GK grew and expanded in Honduras, largely because of our high-performing team. A special thanks to Daphne Sikkafy, GK's first plant manager in the country. Gratitude extends to our first collaborators like Lastenia, Eugenia and Francisco Franco, along with many other friends and business associates. This includes Ing. Rafael Flores, who has been a companion for more than twenty years.

I want to acknowledge the dedication of GK's long-term staff, whose hard work has been key to GK's success in the region and beyond. A nod of appreciation goes to Adrian Hernandez, CEO of GK's fiber and yarn division; Gustavo Raudales, CEO of GK's real estate division; Alfredo Flores, CEO of GK Mexico; Luis Mejia, executive vice president in GK's textile division; Saleem Suriya, associate in Florida; Kathia Yacaman, executive vice president of marketing and sales; Andrea Duarte, GK's Corporate HR Director; and Rose Mary Sabat, the administrations manager at GVIP. Efforts to improve conditions and the well-being of citizens in Honduras and beyond are possible because of the steadfast work of Georgina Barahona and her entire team. I would be remiss not to include our engineering teams, construction teams, yarn and textile plants management teams, and our entire labor force.

There have been so many kindhearted and lovely people in Honduras who welcomed me with open arms. Because of their graciousness, I became a permanent citizen of Honduras. This land and its people have become my own.

My partners Tom Friedland and the late Randy Kogan accompanied me to Campeche, Mexico, and together they believed in opening the first industrial company as a joint venture with GK in a remote and unknown territory where a sewing machine—and how it functioned—were novelties. More than twenty years later, we are still growing and have provided direct jobs to more than four thousand people in the state of Campeche. Randy spent ample time with Alfredo Flores, CEO of GK Mexico, and his team to refine training programs. As a result of his work, we developed programs to help workers excel in their careers and improve their quality of life. Our growth and positive trajectory are due, in large part, to Randy's passion and commitment to both the textile business and the people of Campeche. At GK we are thankful for both Randy and his family.

So many individuals contributed to the creation of this book. In the US I owe deep gratitude to the time and attention of Andy

Warlick, chairman and owner of Parkdale Mills; Bob Humphreys, chairman and owner of Delta Apparel; David Miller, GK sales and marketing division; Eric Miller, president of Rideau Potomac Strategy Group; Kenneth Frankel, law professor based in Toronto, Canada; Sandy Friedland, journalist; Zaffar Tabani, CEO of Tabani Group; and Mark Mertens, owner of A4.

I want to thank attorneys Roger Marine, Jose Ramon Paz, Selvin Lopez, and Tomas Nasser as friends who have been steadfast in their support for me and GK in legal matters in Honduras and the region for over two decades. In Honduras a special thanks goes to Karim Qubain, president of the Consulate Association in San Pedro Sula; Edgardo Dumas, managing partner of Bufete Dumas y Asoc.; José Martín Chicas, president of Inmsa Argo International; Joaquin Muñoz, attorney at Bufete Muñoz Figueroa y Asoc.; Oscar Galeano, general manager of Plásticos Gámoz; Oscar Paz, director of 18 de Noviembre School in Armenta; Mary Ann de Kafati, president of the Ruth Paz Burn and Pediatric Hospital and Ruth Paz Foundation; Romulo Emiliani, auxiliary bishop emeritus of San Pedro Sula, Honduras; Mohamed Riahi, regional director of Coficab; Salman Saif, general manager of Honduras Spinning Mills; Roger Valladares, president of Universidad Tecnológica de Honduras; Daisy Pastor Fasquelle, general manager of Seaboard Marine; Luis Larach, president of Hotel Copantl and CEAL; Mateo Yibrin, president of CADELGA and Cohep; Kenia Lima, owner of ZaGo Solutions; Lenin Palencia, owner of Grupo Amcresa; Claudia Mejia, executive assistant.

I want to express my heartfelt appreciation to those who contributed to the book in Campeche: Ivan Escalante Flores, director of real estate development; Hugo Alfredo Rojas Arias, CFO of GK's Mexico division; Noelia Dávila Midence, plant manager; Marvin Fúnez, director of manufacturing; Teresa Cordoba Escobar, human resources manager; Antonio Zamora Gonzalez, plant manager; Hugo Rojas, financial director; Laura Hernandez Gonzalez, chief of Medline; Nohemi Ake Chable, legal representative at Palomar; Mike Pope, consultant at Medline; and Carlos Mouriño, president of the corporate at GES.

I treasure the bonds with my dear friends Arturo May, Eduardo Martinez, Jorge Manos, Carlos Borges, Raul Pozos Lanz, Marco Marrufo, Javier Cú, Tirzo Garcia, Juan José Casanova, and Pablo and Gabriel Escalante in Campeche. I'd also like to thank my close companions Don Pedro Gutierrez and Enrique Nadal in Tabasco, Bernardo Cueto and Mauricio Merino in the Yucatan Peninsula, and many other friends across Mexico.

A special gesture of gratitude goes to former governors of the state of Campeche, Jorge Carlos Hurtado and Antonio Gonzalez, and the former governor of the state of Quintana Roo Carlos Joaquin.

I want to acknowledge the efforts of Nawaz Akhtar, the GK general manager at Latin Textile in our Dubai operation. He and his team have been responsible for supporting our companies in Central America and Mexico for more than three decades.

I would like to include my gratitude to our partners in Agro Business, Mr. Felix Castillo of Recas (Honduras) and Mr. Say Kiat Au of Rajawali Seroja International. A note of thanks is due to Mr. Abbas Habib, the chairman of the Bank Al-Habib, and Mr. Guillermo Bueso, chairman of Banco Atlántida Group. Kind regards to Mrs. Maria Selman of Banco del Pais, Mr. Mohammed Habib of Habib Bank AZ Zurich, and the many friends with whom we work on initiatives around the world, ranging from healthcare to education and other nonprofit sectors.

I am eternally grateful to God for the blessings in my life. Everything that I am today I owe to him.

HOW TO GET INVOLVED

HEALTHCARE

EDUCATION

SUSTAINABILITY

INNOVATION

If you are interested in expanding your business operations in fragile economies, reach out to us for any help or advice you need.

- ☑ **Corporations who want to expand their business.**
- ☑ **Corporations who want to collaborate with GK Foundation.**

If you are an individual and would like to get involved and make a change in the world, we are here to assist you.

- ☑ **Any individual who wishes to dedicate his or her time and services to support needed communities in these regions.**

A MESSAGE FROM YUSUF:

I wish to inspire individuals, professionals, innovators, entrepreneurs, business leaders, large companies, and small companies to invest in sustainable business in under-developed countries.

But I do not only wish to inspire, but also to be a resource for advice and assistance.

If you are a medical doctor who wishes to go to Honduras to offer medical assistance, we can provide logistics, take you to the most needed places, and look after your well-being, all at no cost. If you are a teacher and wish to spend two weeks in our schools, we will do the same. If you are an entrepreneur who would like to expand or open a business, we can provide advice and support.

At GK, we are available to help you navigate and accomplish your own personal and business objectives and to make the world a better place for all.